More Challenges for the Delusional

Peter Murphy's Prompts and the Writing They Inspired

Edited by
Ona Gritz & Daniel Simpson

Prompts by
Peter Murphy

First Edition 2018 ©Peter E. Murphy
All rights reserved.

ISBN: 978-1-939728-15-9
Diode Editions
Doha, Qatar

Design & layout: Law Alsobrook
Ordering & contact information: http://www.diodeeditions.com

Contents

Poetry

Fiction

Nonfiction

Foreword

It's been six years since *Challenges for the Delusional* was published and five years since its second printing. Needless to say, I am thrilled at its success as both a book of writing prompts and an anthology of poems.

This second volume, *More Challenges for the Delusional*, is not just more of the same. It reflects the growth of Murphy Writing—now part of Stockton University—by including prompts, poems, and prose not only from the Winter Poetry & Prose Getaway, but also from our other retreats held in various locations in New Jersey, New Hampshire, Scotland, Spain, and Wales. These prompts are designed for writers of fiction, nonfiction, and poetry to stretch their creative muscles and write what they didn't know they could write.

In his essay "The Figure a Poem Makes," Robert Frost writes, "No surprise for the writer, no surprise for the reader." Inspired by this remarkable poet, I encourage you to surprise yourself as you work with each prompt. From personal experience, I have found that the surprise may not happen until I've written a few dozen drafts.

I am grateful to Ona Gritz and Daniel Simpson for their hard work and careful editing in putting together this book. I offer my gratitude to Patty Paine and Law Alsobrook of Diode Editions for publishing it. And, of course, we couldn't do what we do without you, the thousands of poets and writers who have participated in our retreats and those who contributed to this collection.

Enjoy the selection of poems and prose, use the prompts to exhaustion, and Write On!

– Peter E. Murphy

Introduction

Late one winter morning—January 15, 2005 to be exact—I sat on a rumpled bed in an unfamiliar hotel room in Cape May, New Jersey, and tried to write a poem on the subject of *home*. More specifically, a poem about home in which *I explore or discover something beyond or beneath the obvious good and bad of it*. I had all of an hour and a half left to do this, after which I was to bring whatever I came up with to a workshop led by one of my literary heroes.

Refer to, include, swipe, steal, amend, or argue one or more of the quotations above, the instructions read. These included "Home is the place where, when you have to go there / They have to take you in" from Robert Frost and "There's no place like home" from Dorothy in *The Wizard of Oz*.

About a year earlier, I'd had a birthday that felt especially significant because I'd reached exactly half the age my mother had been when she died. This could be my midpoint as well, I noted, which led me to ask myself what, if anything, I wanted to change about my life.

The answer was clear and immediate: I was a writer—I had an MFA, a few poems in literary journals, a published children's book, and another under contract—but I hardly ever wrote.

There were good reasons for this. I was a single mother. I had a full-time day job as a librarian. My writing desk was in an apartment on a noisy city street, and I shared that apartment with an even noisier seven-year-old boy.

I thought of all I'd hoped to have accomplished by that point on my life's calendar—the many books written, the prizes won. Of course, I fell short. Everyone does when taking measurements like these. But the deeper truth was that when I didn't make time to write I felt edgy and unsatisfied. My thoughts lost their clarity. My days felt frittered away.

I considered applying to one of those rarified artist colonies that provide a secluded cabin or a room in a stately mansion in which to work. But such residencies, I knew, required many weeks away, and that wasn't something I could manage, given the library's vacation schedule or the young child who needed me at home.

Instead, I did my best with what I had. I downloaded a white noise player so that pounding rain in a recorded loop drowned out the sirens and car alarms outside my apartment. I took a later shift at work so I'd have an extra uninterrupted hour or two in the morning. I turned down lunch dates with friends on the weekends my son was at his dad's. It was a start, but too often my ideas arrived slowly, or the language sounded clunky or didn't say much. And because those blocks of time I'd carved out for myself all came at a cost, I felt guilty for taking them unless the muse cooperated and words fell with beauty and significance from my pen.

Muse-inspired hours. Beauty. Significance. Guilt. A theme was emerging, but in those first weeks and months after my midlife birthday reckoning, I couldn't see it. I didn't realize that my perfectionism was what was getting in my way.

I learned about the Winter Poetry & Prose Getaway by googling a favorite poet of mine: Stephen Dunn. He taught a workshop at this annual conference that took place over the Martin Luther King, Jr. holiday weekend and was just a few hours' drive from where I lived. *Perfect*, I thought. *A writer's retreat brief enough to fit into my already overfull life.* A chance to study with a writer whose work I loved—something I hadn't had the privilege of doing since grad school when, ironically, I was just about half the age I'd recently reached.

The Winter Getaway offers a series of daily generative workshops. The way it works for poetry participants is this: After breakfast, we gather in an otherwise empty banquet hall for a reading of poems that share a common theme. Following the reading, we discuss the poems with the others seated at our table until, finally, we're handed a brightly colored sheet of paper with our assignment: *Write a poem about* **Home** *in which you explore or discover something beyond or beneath the obvious good and bad of it...*

Back on that morning in 2005, when I was new to these rituals, I read the prompt and felt a distinct blend of excitement and dread. Around me, people gathered their folders, notebooks, and steaming to-go cups. We were to meet again in two hours for lunch, having handed in our completed poems for photocopying. I drifted toward the elevator wondering how, in such a short amount of time, I could possibly write something worthwhile enough to bring to a workshop led by Stephen Dunn.

As though hearing my thoughts, Peter Murphy, the founder and facilitator of the program, leaned into his microphone.

"Now, go write a shitty first draft," he said. "Anyone can do that, right?"

Upstairs, I placed the *Recharging My Batteries* sign on the knob and closed myself in my room. I then spent a good ten or more of my precious minutes pacing from dresser to bed to window and back again, muttering the word *Home* and glancing nervously at the clock. All the while, Peter's suggestion flickered at the edge of my mind, and I did my best to bat it away. I didn't want to write a shitty draft. I wanted to…what? Write a masterpiece? Impress everyone with my extraordinary talent? Well… Yeah.

I laughed, recognizing not just the hubris of my goal, but also the pure ridiculousness of it. All any of us had time for before lunch that day was a first draft, which is, after all, a kind of playground–a place to explore and experiment. I knew that, or at least I once did. Back in my grad school days in New York, I used to trick myself into starting new poems by pulling out my notebook when I rode the subway. There, on the bustling, unpredictable train, I had the freeing sense that I wasn't seriously working, but rather, just killing time until I reached my stop.

Here's something else about those often-fruitful subway writing sessions. They were brief. Thirty minutes here, another twenty later in the week. Maybe there was genius in the tight schedule of the Getaway. We had just enough time to write, but not enough to then fret over our drafts' imperfections. I pictured the little placard I'd dangled from the doorknob minutes earlier. Its first purpose, of course, was to let housekeeping know that this wasn't the time to change the linens and replace the soap. But maybe it could also serve as a reminder to leave my censorious inner critic at the door.

Finally, I dropped, cross-legged, onto my unmade bed and reread the prompt: *Refer to, include, swipe, steal, amend, or argue one or more of the quotations.* Along with Robert Frost and Dorothy, there was a brief quote from poet Elinor Mattern, whom I later learned was a longtime Getaway regular: *"Home is a splintered boat."* I thought about my noisy apartment and my little boy a hundred and fifty miles away. These days our home felt loving and whole, but there was definitely a time when it had seemed splintered, when the extraordinary gift of a newborn child was juxtaposed against a marriage that was in serious trouble. *Something beyond or beneath the obvious good and bad of it…* From outside in the hall, I could hear the hum and bump of a vacuum. A door slammed. Someone laughed too loudly. None of that mattered. I was also beginning to hear a poem.

Home, I Say

From the wash, I pull a shirt
the size of a dinner napkin,
stretch the opening at the neck
so as not to frighten him
with too long a moment blinded by cloth.
So many mistakes I can make, and I do.
The worst, catching a bit of his skin
between the locked halves of a snap.
Cries can be stoppered most times
by the sudden milk my body makes,
suck and swallow the only sound
beside the rhythmic thump of our chair.
Blue eyes drinking me in, I feel
compelled to name things for him.
Window and *bear*. *Sunlight* and *reading lamp*.
Home, I say, as though this place
is not a splintered boat.
And, *Daddy*, as though this person
is not already taking leave.

Meanwhile, in other rooms and on other floors, writers had their own encounters with the various ingredients of the morning's assignment. *Surprise yourself*, Peter had added at the bottom of the page. *Do not settle for what you already know*. A tall order under ordinary circumstances, but the wonder of Peter's prompts is that they send us off in new directions, helping us create work we wouldn't otherwise come up with, yet that's entirely our own.

Here is another example of a poem about *home* written by someone who was also new to the Getaway that year:

Living with Others

Last night as I was leaving,
Animal Control was just arriving
to collect the squirrel from the baited trap.
Eight now in two weeks.

While I'm sleeping, showering, listening to Brahms,
they're up there gnawing, chasing, crying
in what sounds like sexy pleasure.
I don't know where they're coming in,
or how they're getting out.

I had a wife once, and some days
she chewed her way through my exterior.
On others, I flung the door wide open.

Maybe I should just return the cage,
learn to live with rodents
who, after all, only want to do
the things we say we honor:
make a stable home, raise their young.

But this is all wrong;
ex-wives and squirrels are not the same.
Still, last time, the wires that got crossed,
the burning,
the length of silence afterward.

When, a few hours later, the man sitting beside me in Stephen Dunn's workshop shared that poem with the group, I was struck by both the craft and the heart of it, by how those interloping squirrels, held up against the speaker's failed marriage, created a deeper understanding of what it means to make a home.

There were ten of us at the table and, as we made our way around the circle, Stephen offered each of us feedback that was both exacting and generous. He also talked about his own writing practice, offered his perspective on the components of good writing, and read us poems he loved.

It was an intense three hours, but I came away from the workshop feeling energized. Writing is a solitary act, which is something I actually love about it, but I'd forgotten how invigorating it can also be to spend time with other practitioners—to hear what they're reading and working on and thinking about. I understood then that I'd given myself a tremendous gift by coming to the Winter Getaway, but what I didn't yet know was that I had stumbled upon a community of writers that would soon be central to my life. Stephen and Peter would become not just mentors to me but, along with several others I met that weekend, good friends.

As for the author of "Living With Others," whom I'd immediately liked for his gentle manner and thoughtful observations, he is now my husband and the co-editor of this book. It was only after Dan and I began work on the manuscript that we made the connection: we each met the person with whom we now share a home on the very day we grappled with the subject of *home* in our first Getaway poems. Such is the magic and alchemy of a Peter Murphy Prompt.

This is not to say that if you write from the prompts in this book you'll find the community you most need and meet the love of your life. But a shift will happen, at least in the way you approach an empty Word document or a clean notebook page. It will no longer seem so blank.

Dan tells me he considers Peter's prompts *friendly dares*. "It's not like Peter is saying *I bet you can't*," he explains, "but rather, *See if you can*."

Peter himself claims they're all challenges for the delusional.

I think of a former library coworker who once described to me why she loved preparing meals from recipe books. "It's like cooking with a friend," she said. For me, working from one of Peter's prompts is like collaborating with a friend–one whose mind makes surprising leaps and connections, and who quickly gets mine to do the same.

❧

The Winter Poetry & Prose Getaway is now twice as old as it was when Dan and I met there in 2005. This new collection celebrates the conference's 25th year. In addition to prompts for generating poetry, fiction, and nonfiction, we've included a sampling of works that were born and shaped at Murphy Writing's various retreats. Some are by faculty, but most are by participants. You'll find poems, stories, and essays set in supermarkets and dime stores, classrooms, hair salons, cars, and kitchens. Narrators speak from atop an exam table and from a high school running track, while swimming, walking along the shore, and (omnisciently) taking us on a mission to rescue a crew lost at sea. There are pieces that are political, spiritual, humorous, and surreal. The authors tackle subjects such as loss, sex, time, marriage, belonging, and forgiveness. We've included this selection in part to *kvell*–look at what those one-time shitty first drafts have evolved into! More than that, these samples are here to do what all good writing does: inform, challenge, nourish, connect, and inspire.

– Ona Gritz

How to Use This Book

Many of the prompts in this book started out as prompts for poetry alone. In recent years, however, Peter Murphy has been creating prompts that could work across all three genres: poetry, fiction, and nonfiction. To provide consistency for this book, Ona Gritz and I have gone back and adapted the poetry-only prompts to have parallels for the other two genres. Although I have attended Murphy Writing Getaways primarily as a poet, I believe that what I've learned from using Peter's poetry prompts can be readily applied to writing fiction and nonfiction.

How to Use the Prompts

I urge you to approach the prompts in this book in one of two ways:

1. Simply take them as they come; just start at the beginning and work your way through.

2. Open to a random prompt. If it's one you've used before, try again until you land on a new one.

In either approach, once you arrive at a new prompt, commit to it. If, after the first half hour, it feels like your writing is going nowhere, too bad. Even if you still have a blank page or screen in front of you, stick with it anyway.

Why be so draconian about this? Because what works so well about Peter's prompts is that, by restricting you, they often lead you to surprise yourself. Occasionally, you'll read a prompt and think, "Oh, my God, this prompt was made for me." Consider it a gift and enjoy it. At least as often, you'll read one and think, "This leaves me completely cold; I have nothing to say on this prompt." That's a different kind of gift. Since most of us don't wake up every morning inspired and with unlimited writing time, prompts like that provide the best practice for writing under real life conditions. The clock and the restrictive prompt grind against each other like tectonic plates creating friction and, if you're lucky, a little earthquake. The clock keeps ticking, and you dawdle, doodle, scratch your armpit again, and grab a piece or three of chocolate, then press on, write another line, take a bigger risk out of desperation, and maybe break through to something you had no idea you would say.

Of course, sometimes it doesn't quite happen that way, and what you get is more like a mud pie trying to look like a poem. That's still a good day's work. You might have enough to revise into a more successful piece another day. Maybe all you'll get is a decent line or two to seed another piece. You'll also have gotten hands-on experience with seeing why something didn't work, which will tune you to better decisions next time. Ultimately, you can't lose. If nothing else, you've exercised your writing muscles. The more exercised those muscles get, the less you'll have to rely on outside inspiration.

Think of the prompt as your partner in a relationship. Better yet, your partner in an arranged marriage. Our popular culture tends to focus more on the excitement of romantic love than the discipline and practical decisions of long-term, day-to-day love. Something similar can happen when we write. We work on something for an hour and find ourselves just plodding along, not feeling very inspired. So we think, "Maybe if I try a different poem, start over, I'll have a better time of it." I won't say that this never works, but I believe that if we make a habit of ditching prompts when the going gets tough, we're likely to become better at flirting with writing than being a committed partner. So stick with the prompt. Hey, it's only a couple of hours, not a lifetime.

Once you get that first draft written, you don't have to be—in fact, you shouldn't be—wedded to it in its current form. If modifying or deleting something that got into your work via the prompt will improve the work, by all means, don't act with loyalty to it just because it came from the prompt. At this point, your loyalty is to the work, not the prompt.

Secrets, Lies, and...Ponies

Included in every one of Peter Murphy's poetry prompts, you can find these words: "Tell a secret and tell a lie and never tell anyone which is which." As Peter says in the introduction to the first volume of *Challenges For the Delusional*, telling a secret creates a sense of intimacy with readers that will make them want to keep reading. As for telling a lie, it gives poets a simple reminder to allow their imaginations to run free. Since fiction writers have permission to make up everything, they have no contract with the reader regarding the truth. Of course, there's nothing stopping them from borrowing a secret or a truth from their own lives to enrich their stories, and we encourage this from time to time in the fiction prompts. Certainly, memoirists can also benefit from pushing themselves to reveal secrets, not only those they were not supposed to share with the outside world or other family members, but also those which they had kept from themselves until they started to write. For some, in fact, revealing secrets is at the heart of their work.

While memoirists have an unspoken contract with the reader not to out-and-out lie about what happened, they do have a certain amount of leeway when it comes to recreating dialogue or speculating about what happened in places where there are gaps in memory or factual knowledge. In her personal essay "What Lies Beneath," Ona Gritz tells of a time when she sat on the living room floor, while her father spoke to another adult about thugs who think nothing of breaking into houses and slitting the throats of their inhabitants. "I was six at the time," she writes, "coloring a picture of a pony in a field on the coffee table next to where my father sat, puffing his sweet-smelling pipe. He didn't mean to scare me; he believed children paid no attention when adults spoke to one another."

"That's amazing," I said, when she first read that to me. "I'm not surprised that you remember what your father was talking about, given how shocking it was to you, but that you remember exactly what you were doing—and not only that you were coloring at the coffee table, but that it was a pony in a field. It's that pony that convinces me that I can trust the accuracy of the narrator's memory. It's that pony that makes the incident so vivid and real."

"That's funny," Ona said. "I made up the pony. I mean, it's the kind of thing I might have been doing when that happened, but I wouldn't swear to it. I just know it felt right, that it was emotionally true to that moment."

That's how complicated memoir's relationship to the truth can get. Another case in point: I just made up that little bit of dialogue between Ona and me. It's close to what we said, accurate with regard to the overall tenor of that conversation, but I don't remember the actual dialogue word for word. As memoirists, we constantly have to navigate that border between memory and imagination, and we all draw different lines. The term *making ponies* has become shorthand between Ona and me for inviting creativity in to help flesh out a vague recollection. She is more likely just to make the pony because it's emotionally true and let it do the work of transporting you into the moment. I'm more likely to tell you that I'm doing so.

Since this is ultimately a personal decision, we have made occasional suggestions in the nonfiction prompts to help you experiment and find your own way of handling the truth.

Getting the Most from the Poetry and Prose in This Book

While we hope you will enjoy the poems and prose pieces included here for their own sake, we think you might also find them to be prompts in their own right, stirring up new ideas and connections as any good literature can. After all, reading is an essential part of good writing. To write without reading is like walking into a room where people have been conversing for millennia and to start talking without taking the time to listen to what others have been saying. That's why, at Murphy Writing retreats, we always start by reading.

May you find benefit in this book, and may you be happy in your work, both the reading and the writing!

– Daniel Simpson

Prompts

Hide and Seek

5th Annual Shore Thing Writing Getaway — 2017

....

Look wise, say nothing, and grunt. Speech was given to conceal thought.
— Sir William Osler

What are you hiding? No one ever asks that.
— Sarah Vowell

The secret to creativity is knowing how to hide your sources.
— Albert Einstein

....

Assignments

Fiction

Write a story in which one character hides something that another character wants.

Nonfiction/Memoir

Write about a time you either hid something from someone, or you uncovered something that had been hidden from you. Allow your imagination to wander in and help with dialogue and other partially remembered details.

Poetry

Write a poem in which something hidden is revealed. Tell a secret and tell a lie and never tell anyone which is which.

Requirements for All

1. Set your writing in a clearly recognizable place.

2. Use at least 6 words that are hiding inside other words (See Appendix A).

Challenge for the Delusional

Mention your left foot and a primary number.

Surprise yourself! Do not settle for what you already know!

The Hard Way

7th Annual International Writing Retreat: Get Away to Write: Scotland — 2016

Appreciate your mistakes for what they are: precious life lessons that can only be learned the hard way. Unless it's a fatal mistake, which, at least, others can learn from.

— Al Franken

Absolute certainty is not something I strive for anymore. I've learned the hard way that destiny usually looks upon our most strident convictions with amusement, or perhaps even pity.

— Elizabeth Gilbert

An intellectual says a simple thing in a hard way. An artist says a hard thing in a simple way.

— Charles Bukowski

Assignments

Fiction

Write a story in which a character learns something the hard way. Sneak in a detail or two from your real life.

Nonfiction/Memoir

Write an essay about something you learned the hard way. Reveal a well-kept secret.

Poetry

Write a poem about a painful learning experience. Tell a secret and tell a lie and never tell anyone which is which.

Requirements for All

1. Experiment with sound and imagery you would not ordinarily use.

2. Mention an item of clothing and a fruit.

Challenge for the Delusional

Make a door, dog, doctor, dance, or drapes an essential part of your piece.

Surprise yourself! Do not settle for what you already know!

You Animal, You!

1st Annual Writing in the Pines Retreat — 2015

❧❦❧

Man is the Only Animal that Blushes. Or needs to.

— Mark Twain

Perhaps I am a bear, or some hibernating animal underneath, for the instinct to be half asleep all winter is so strong in me.

— Anne Morrow Lindbergh

My favorite animal is steak.

— Fran Lebowitz

❧❦❧

Assignments

Fiction

Create an animal narrator that observes and comments on the humans in your story.

Nonfiction/Memoir

Write an essay that uses your relationship to an animal to reveal something unusual about your human self.

Poetry

Write a poem that uses an animal to reveal something unusual about your human self. Tell a secret and tell a lie and never tell anyone which is which.

Requirements for All

1. Begin with a subordinating conjunction.*

2. Steal interesting language from a fortune cookie or two (See Appendix B).

Challenge for the Delusional

End your piece with a question, actual, or rhetorical.

Surprise yourself! Do not settle for what you already know!

*after, although, as, if, because, since, unless, as if, as though, before, even if, even though, if only, in order that, now that, once, rather than, so that, than, that, though, till, until, when, whenever, where, whereas, wherever, while, why.

A Sense of Place
5th Annual International Writing Retreat: Dylan Thomas' Wales — 2014

Maybe you had to leave in order to miss a place; maybe you had to travel to figure out how beloved your starting point was.

— Jodi Picoult

There is no there there.

— Gertrude Stein

London is a language. I guess all places are.

— David Mitchell

Assignments

Fiction

Have a character return to her/his/their hometown after a long absence. Explore how both the person and the place have and have not changed. Include something true from your own life.

Nonfiction/Memoir

Write a personal essay about a place that is different from how you remember it, either because it has changed with time, or because you have. Reveal a secret.

Poetry

Write a poem about a place you thought you knew that surprised and/or changed you. Tell a secret and tell a lie and never tell anyone which is which.

Requirements for All

1. Begin with a line or two of description.

2. Include at least one detail from a place you have lived and another from a place where you have visited.

3. In your descriptions, make sure you appeal to senses other than sight.

Challenge for the Delusional

Mention a historical person or event that may or may not have affected a character, friend, relative, or ancestor.

Surprise yourself! Yeah! Yeah! Yeah!

Going Mobile

1st Annual Quickie Writing Getaway — 2010

. . . .

When you come to a fork in the road, take it.

— Yogi Berra

I hate the outdoors. To me the outdoors is where the car is.

— Will Durst

Someday we'll look back on this moment and plow into a parked car.

— Evan Davis

. . . .

Assignments

Fiction

Place two or more characters who are in conflict inside a car and don't let them out until something changes between them.

Nonfiction/Memoir

Write about something significant that happened in a car, or that has something to do with a car (first kiss, first accident, driver training, etc. Who knows? Maybe that kiss was your first accident...) Use the places where you don't have all the facts to your creative advantage.

Poetry

Write a poem set in or about an automobile. Tell a secret and tell a lie and never tell anyone which is which.

Requirements for All

1. Grapple with something that's been bothering you.

2. Include vivid images that appeal to the five senses.

Challenge for the Delusional

If you tend toward narrative, fracture it. If you tend toward lyric, experiment with story.

My Word

21st Annual Winter Poetry & Prose Getaway — 2014

When ideas fail, words come in very handy.
— Johann Wolfgang von Goethe

Words are, of course, the most powerful drug used by mankind.
— Rudyard Kipling

*The difference between the right word and the almost right word
is the difference between lightning and a lightning bug.*
— Mark Twain

Assignments

Fiction

Write a flash fiction piece in which two characters argue over the exact wording of a document that is important to both of them. Emphasize one word that is at the crux of their dispute. Limit your piece to 750 words.

Nonfiction/Memoir

Write a flash piece riffing on a single word that was somehow defining for you at a particular point in your life. Limit your piece to 750 words.

Poetry

Write a postcard-size poem celebrating a word. Tell a secret and tell a lie and never tell anyone which is which.

Requirements for All

1. Steal language and images from a postcard or two, either from your personal collection, or from our virtual postcard collection at *murphywriting.com/anthology*.

2. Be audacious!

Challenge for the Delusional

Choose your word from one of the postcards.

Vacation Time

1st Annual Shore Thing Writing Getaway — 2013

❧

For a while we pondered whether to take a vacation or get a divorce. We decided that a trip to Bermuda is over in two weeks, but a divorce is something you always have.

— Woody Allen

No man needs a vacation so much as the man who has just had one.

— Elbert Hubbard

The prospect of a long day at the beach makes me panic. There is no harder work I can think of than taking myself off to somewhere pleasant, where I am forced to stay for hours and 'have fun.'

— Phillip Lopate

Assignments

Fiction

Two characters are on their way to Atlantic City. Write a dialogue-driven story in which one character feels wronged by the other and wants some form of reparation. What is the balance between Justice and Mercy?

Nonfiction/Memoir

Write about a vacation that went worse (or better) than expected. Discover something you didn't know you knew. Be both truthful and merciful toward yourself and others as you write.

Poetry

Draw on a vacation or a journey to write a poem about Mercy. Tell a secret and tell a lie and never tell anyone which is which.

Requirements for All

1. Begin your first draft with the word "Although."

2. Drop a brand name or two into your writing.

3. Use images, sounds, and smells associated with your vacation's setting.

Challenge for the Delusional

Repeat a word, phrase, or sentence you've already used as your last sentence or line.

Dear Me

⸎

*I think on-stage nudity is disgusting, shameful, and damaging to all
things American. But if I were 22 with a great body, it would be
artistic, tasteful, patriotic, and a progressive religious experience.*

— Shelley Winters

Age is an issue of mind over matter. If you don't mind, it doesn't matter.

— Mark Twain

Boys will be boys, and so will a lot of middle-aged men.

— Kin Hubbard

⸎

Assignments

Fiction

While going through the effects of a deceased family member,
a character discovers a letter or note that calls into question
everything she thought she knew about that person.

> *Variation*: A letter from beyond the grave (should we say from the Dead
> Letter office?) mysteriously appears in a character's mailbox.

Nonfiction/Memoir

Write about a letter that dramatically changed your life.

> *Variation*: Write the letter you most wish you had written.

Poetry

If you are younger than fifty, write an epistolary poem to your eighty-
year-old-self. If you are older than fifty, address one to your twenty-
year-old-self. If you are exactly fifty, you decide. Tell a secret and tell a
lie and never tell anyone which is which.

> *Variation*: Lie about your age and address your poem to
> your other self.

Requirements for All

1. Ask an important question.

2. Include three or four words from the list of random words
   (See Appendix C).

Challenge for the Delusional

Write it as a dramatic monologue from the point of view of someone
whose gender identity is different from your own.

Historically Speaking

2nd Annual Writing in the Pines Retreat — 2016

* * *

If Beethoven had been killed in a plane crash at the age of 22, it would have changed the history of music...and of aviation.

— Tom Stoppard

For most of history, Anonymous was a woman.

— Virginia Woolf

There's an old saying about those who forget history. I don't remember it, but it's good.

— Stephen Colbert

* * *

Assignments

Fiction

Write a short story told from the point of view of a historical persona.

Nonfiction/Memoir

Write about an event of historical significance that happened in your lifetime. Where were you? In what ways were you affected?

Poetry

Write a poem that uses a historical event to reveal something surprising about your personal history. Tell a secret and tell a lie and never tell anyone which is which.

Variation: Have a historical persona narrate your poem.

Requirements for All

1. Begin with a question or two.

2. Include a monument, a street name, and a mode of transportation.

Challenge for the Delusional

Mention the title of a song that was popular the year you were born.

Hold a Mirror Up to Fear

21st Annual Winter Poetry & Prose Getaway — 2014

I write entirely to find out what I'm thinking, what I'm looking at, what I see and what it means. What I want and what I fear.

—Joan Didion

The optimist proclaims that we live in the best of all possible worlds; and the pessimist fears this is true.

—Branch Cabell

Fear is a question.

—Marilyn Ferguson

Assignments

Fiction

Place a character in front of a mirror at the start of a story about fear.

Nonfiction/Memoir

Write an essay that touches on something you are afraid to write about. Include the image of a mirror somewhere in the piece.

Poetry

Place a mirror in a poem about something you fear. Tell a secret and tell a lie and never tell anyone which is which.

Requirements for All

1. Begin your first draft with "If instead..." You can change it later.

2. Use a word or two from the Oxford English Dictionary list (See Appendix D).

Challenge for the Delusional

Make it humorous.

Oh, God

3rd Annual Quickie Writing Getaway — 2012

❧❧❧

It is the final proof of God's omnipotence that he need not exist in order to save us.

— Peter De Vries

God is not dead but alive and well and working on a much less ambitious project.

— Anonymous

If you want to know what God thinks of money, just look at the people he gave it to.

— Dorothy Parker

For I have come to turn a man against his father, a daughter against her mother, a daughter-in-law against her mother-in-law—a man's enemies will be the members of his own household.

Matthew 10, 35–36

❧❧❧

Assignments

Fiction

Two lovers, siblings, or close friends are approaching a religious holiday. One believes wholeheartedly in God; the other wholeheartedly does not.

Nonfiction/Memoir

Write about a particular time or event in your own story or your family's when issues around God took center stage. Make it dialogue-driven, but don't worry if you don't remember the exact words that were spoken.

Poetry

Write a poem that uses "God" to think about something much more mundane. Tell a secret and tell a lie and never tell anyone which is which.

Requirements for All

1. Mention a kitchen appliance, a hotel chain, and a movie you have not seen.

2. Use a body part in an especially inventive way.

Challenge for the Delusional

Include an argument or quotation from a theologian or other religious figure such as Moses, Thomas Aquinas, Rumi, Mary Baker Eddy, Martin Buber, Mother Teresa, etc.

My Bad

༈

Men are taught to apologize for their weaknesses, women for their strengths.

— Lois Wyse

If you even dream of beating me you'd better wake up and apologize.

— Muhammad Ali

If God doesn't punish America, He'll have to apologize to Sodom and Gomorrah.

— Billy Graham

༈

Assignments

Fiction

A character refuses to apologize to her/his/their lover for doing something stupid. Sneak in something factually accurate about yourself.

Nonfiction/Memoir

Write about an apology (or lack of an apology) that went wrong. If you're missing some facts, fill them in as best you can with what might have been true and tells the "Greater Truth."

Poetry

Write a poem in which you apologize for something you may or may not have done. Tell a secret and tell a lie and never tell anyone which is which.

> *Challenging Variation for "Delusional" Poets:*
> Make it formal: a sonnet, ode, villanelle, or sestina.

Requirements for All

1. Mention the moon, a piece of furniture, and a tool.

2. Steal interesting language from a fortune cookie or two (See Appendix B).

Challenge for the Delusional

Write as a series of epistles: letters, emails, texts, etc.

Something Borrowed

5th Annual International Writing Retreat: Dylan Thomas' Wales — 2014

I don't read much of what I write because I worry about unintentionally borrowing something.

— Kelley Armstrong

Borrowing is not much better than begging; just as lending with interest is not much better than stealing.

— Doris Lessing

I have always played into the belief that you are only ever borrowing the jersey; you never own the jersey because someone has gone before you and there is going to be someone after you, so it's a case of giving the jersey maximum respect.

— Brian O'Driscoll

Assignments

Borrowed Lines for all genres

- After we flew across the country…
- This morning, on the opposite shore of the river…
- The day the tickets arrived…
- A state you must dare not enter…
- I'm sitting in the No Sign bar…

Fiction

Launch a story with one of the borrowed lines (above). You may delete or change it after your first draft.

Nonfiction/Memoir

Begin an essay with one of the borrowed lines (above), changing a word or detail, if necessary, so that it fits your own experience.

Poetry

Write a poem that begins with one of the borrowed lines (above). Feel free to delete or change it after your first draft. Tell a secret and tell a lie and never tell anyone which is which.

Requirements for All

1. Borrow one or two requirements from any of the other prompts.

2. Put something old, something new, or something blue in your piece.

Challenge for the Delusional

Include all three—something old, new, and blue.

Under Advisement

༺ஐஐ༻

If you are a dog and your owner suggests that you wear a sweater, suggest that he wear a tail.

— Fran Lebowitz

༺ஐஐ༻

Assignments

Fiction

Write a piece of flash fiction entitled "The Advisor" whose opening line is "Listen," he said, as he opened his third can of beer. Limit yourself to 750 words.

Nonfiction/Memoir

Write a piece of flash nonfiction where one person gives advice to another, whether it be for better or for worse, timely and crucial, or just one more example of the ridiculously inconsequential advice from outer space that Uncle Farquar loved to give. Limit yourself to 750 words.

Poetry

Write a postcard-size poem addressed to yourself from a persona, human or not, that offers meaningful, humorous, or terrible advice. Fit your poem to the size of a postcard. Tell a secret and tell a lie and never tell anyone which is which.

> *Variation*: Offer advice to a creature that could use it.

Requirements for All

1. Ground your writing in a specific place.

2. Steal language and images from a postcard or two, either from your personal collection, or from our virtual postcard collection at *murphywriting.com/anthology*.

Challenge for the Delusional

Include the capital city of a foreign country and the title of a book or movie.

Take a Stroll

5th Annual Ocean View Getaway — 2010

Everywhere is walking distance if you have the time.

— Steven Wright

My grandmother started walking five miles a day when she was sixty. She's ninety-seven now, and we don't know where the hell she is.

— Ellen DeGeneres

I was walking down the street wearing glasses when the prescription ran out.

— Steven Wright

Assignments

Starting Point for all genres

Go for a walk and take notes on what you see, remember, and imagine. Be specific about what's around you. Include graffiti, street names, types of plants and trees, bridges, people, establishments, etc. Don't forget what comes to you from your other senses—smells from the local bakery, the feel of the gravel path, the sound of a distant plane…

Fiction

Write a story in which a character is starting a new life in a new environment. Include details based on the notes from your walk.

Nonfiction/Memoir

Write an essay that begins where you are now, both in terms of place and phase of life, and then moves backwards in time. Include details based on the notes from your walk.

Poetry

Write a "walking around" poem in present tense using the specifics you gathered on your walk as well as things remembered and imagined. You may consider ending your poem with a memory as Frank O'Hara does in his poem, The Day Lady Died, which you can find on the poetryfoundation.org website. Tell a secret and tell a lie and never tell anyone which is which.

Requirements for All

1. Begin your piece with several lines of pure description.

2. Be bold. Don't worry about writing badly.

Challenge for the Delusional

Instead of a walk, ride a bus, train, ferry, plane, or some other mode of public transportation.

An Important Failure
20th Annual Winter Poetry & Prose Getaway — 2013

꙳꙳꙳

I don't think there is a proper way to celebrate something which makes you happy.

— Matthew Oliphant

If we don't succeed, we run the risk of failure.

— Dan Quayle

My one regret in life is that I am not someone else.

— Woody Allen

꙳꙳꙳

Assignments

Fiction

Write a story in which a character's failure leads to something positive.

Variation: Write a story in which a character's success leads to something negative.

Nonfiction/Memoir

Write about a time you failed at something and wound up glad that you did.

Variation: Write about a time you succeeded at something and wound up sorry that you did.

Poetry

Write a poem that celebrates an important failure. Tell a secret and tell a lie and never tell anyone which is which.

Variation: Write about the downside of success.

Requirements for All

1. Include the word "Darling" in your first draft. Feel free to dump it later.

2. Borrow a line, sentence, or paragraph from a piece of your own writing that you consider a failure.

Challenge for the Delusional

Mention a failure made famous by history or literature.

It's Magic
4th Annual Shore Thing Writing Getaway — 2016

Disbelief in magic can force a poor soul into believing in government and business.

— Tom Robbins

If you see the magic in a fairytale, you can face the future.

— Danielle Steel

Science is magic that works.

— Kurt Vonnegut

Assignments

Fiction

Write a story in which something magical is accepted as normal. Begin with an outrageous claim.

Nonfiction/Memoir

Write about a time you allowed yourself to engage in magical thinking.

Poetry

Include a bird or a fish in a poem that tries to reveal or explain something magical. Tell a secret and tell a lie and never tell anyone which is which.

Requirements for All

1. Begin your first draft with a subordinating conjunction.*

2. Have something that's not supposed to fly, fly.

Challenge for the Delusional

Mention a pungent odor, a primary color, and a fabric such as plastic, leather, satin, or corduroy.

*after, although, as, if, because, since, unless, as if, as though, before, even if, even though, if only, in order that, now that, once, rather than, so that, than, that, though, till, until, when, whenever, where, whereas, wherever, while, why.

Standing Up or Giving Up

2nd Annual Live Free and Write Retreat — 2011

When defeat is inevitable, it is wisest to yield.

— Quintilian

When you relinquish the desire to control your future, you can have more happiness.

— Nicole Kidman

It takes a great deal of bravery to stand up to our enemies, but just as much to stand up to our friends.

— J.K. Rowling

Assignments

Fiction

Write a story in which the characters wrestle with the choice between fighting to change the situation they find themselves in and accepting things as they are. Make your story dialogue-driven and place it in a clearly defined setting.

Nonfiction/Memoir

Write about a time when you decided to fight for something you wanted after nearly giving up, or about a time you accepted defeat after putting up a good fight. Share something you are reluctant to reveal. Include dialogue but don't worry if you don't remember the exact words that were spoken.

Poetry

Write a poem that explores the line between fighting for something and letting go. Tell a secret and tell a lie and never tell anyone which is which.

Requirements for All

1. Refer to a personal totem or a possession that either you or a character cherishes.

2. Attempt a linguistic or structural risk. This means playing with diction, dialect, form, sounds, kaleidoscopic images, fragmented sentences, etc.

Challenge for the Delusional

Include the name of a rock band.

Ordinarily

4th Annual Shore Thing Writing Getaway — 2016

....

A man can stand anything except a succession of ordinary days.
— Johann Wolfgang von Goethe

In the right light, at the right time, everything is extraordinary.
— Aaron Rose

Things happen according to the ordinary course of nature and the ordinary habits of life.
— California Civil Code

Life changes in the instant. The ordinary instant.
— Joan Didion

....

Assignments

Fiction

Write a story in which something unexpected happens on an otherwise ordinary day.

Nonfiction/Memoir

Write an essay in which you describe an unexpected discovery you made on what started as an ordinary day.

Poetry

Write an ode to something ordinary or unexpected. Tell a secret and tell a lie and never tell anyone which is which.

> *Challenging Variation for "Delusional" Poets*: Make it formal: a sonnet, ode, villanelle, or sestina.

Requirements for All

1. Begin with dialogue—a line or two for poetry, a sentence or two for prose.

2. Mention a specific invention or discovery. Consider using one of the "Life-Changing Inventions that were Created by Mistake" (See Appendix E).

Challenge for the Delusional

Write it in the third person.

Weathering Loss

2nd Annual Quickie Writing Getaway — 2011

···

No matter how rich you become, how famous or powerful, when you die the size of your funeral will still pretty much depend on the weather.
— Michael Pritchard

Dear beautiful Spring weather, I miss you. Was it something I said?
— Kim Corbin

Don't knock the weather; nine-tenths of the people couldn't start a conversation if it didn't change once in a while.
— Kin Hubbard

Assignments

Fiction

Drive a storm into a story in which something or someone is devastatingly lost to the protagonist.

Nonfiction/Memoir

Write about an important loss. Recall the weather at the time and reflect on whether it mirrored and enhanced your emotions or contradicted them.

Poetry

Involve the weather in a poem about loss. Tell a secret and tell a lie and never tell anyone which is which.

Requirements for All

1. Avoid sentimentality while striving for sentiment (See Appendix F).

2. Steal language and images from a postcard or two, either from your personal collection, or from our virtual postcard collection at *murphywriting.com/anthology*.

Challenge for the Delusional

Include language from an actual weather report you might read in the newspaper or see on television.

The Afterlife

❦❦❦

What happened to Prufrock after the tea party? To Ishmael when he finally made it back to terra firma? To the speaker and neighbor in Frost's Mending Wall after they finished the job? To Horatio after the death of Hamlet? What became of Fay Wray's character after the death of King Kong? Of Shane after he rode into the sunset?

❦❦❦

Assignments

Fiction

Write a story that imagines the afterlife, as it were, of a famous character from literature or popular culture.

Nonfiction/Memoir

Write about a famous character from literature or popular culture who lives on through her/his/their importance to you.

Poetry

Write a poem that imagines the afterlife, as it were, of a famous character from literature or popular culture. Tell a secret and tell a lie and never tell anyone which is which.

Requirements for All

1. Include a direct quote from your character or famous person of choice.

2. Take a million risks and if you fail, fail brilliantly!

3. Have fun!

Challenge for the Delusional

Include the most bizarre fact that you can discover or invent about your famous character.

Dress It Up

1st Annual Shore Thing Writing Getaway — 2013

⁂

Though I am grateful for the blessings of wealth, it hasn't changed who I am. My feet are still on the ground. I'm just wearing better shoes.
— Oprah Winfrey

Beware of all enterprises that require new clothes.
— Thoreau

Arithmetic is being able to count up to twenty without taking off your shoes.
— Mickey Mouse

⁂

Assignments

Fiction

Include clothing in a story in which someone has either died or is dying. Have a character tell a lie.

Nonfiction/Memoir

Mention an article of clothing in an essay that explores issues around death and dying. See if you can tell a lie in the piece while somehow still telling the truth.

Poetry

Throw some clothing into a poem about death or dying. Tell a secret and tell a lie and never tell anyone which is which.

Requirements for All

1. Begin with a line or two of pure description.

2. Mention a birth, invention, or discovery.

Challenge for the Delusional

Experiment with dialogue, diction, sound, or form.

Equinox
Challenges for the Delusional Launch Reading — 2012

⁂

And there are loners in rural communities who, at the equinox, are said to don new garments and stroll down to the cities, where great beasts await them, fat and docile.
— Louis Aragon

Spring has returned. The Earth is like a child that knows poems.
— Rainer Maria Rilke

Youth is like spring, an over praised season more remarkable for biting winds than genial breezes. Autumn is the mellower season, and what we lose in flowers we more than gain in fruits.
— Samuel Butler

⁂

Assignments

Fiction

Write a story that takes place during the equinox and explores a personal relationship that is out of balance. Sneak something true about yourself into your story. If you tend toward writing in first person, try second or third, and vice versa.

Nonfiction/Memoir

Write about a relationship that is or was out of balance. Refer to, and include images from, a particular season of the year. Approximate the facts, if you have to, in order to tell the "Greater Truth."

Poetry

Include the equinox in a poem that explores a personal relationship that is out of balance. For an example, read Elizabeth Alexander's poem Equinox, which can be found on the poetryfoundation.org website. Tell a secret, tell a lie, and never tell anyone which is which.

Requirements for All

1. Begin with a line or two of pure description.

2. Mention an insect, a flower, or a waterfowl.

3. Include a random detail from "Maryland Facts and Trivia" (See Appendix G).

Challenge for the Delusional

Mention the name of your favorite or least favorite celebrity.

Object Lesson

4th Annual Ocean View Getaway — 2009

~~~

Never fight an inanimate object.

— P. J. O'Rourke

No ideas but in things.

— William Carlos Williams

Inanimate objects are classified scientifically into three major categories—those that don't work, those that break down, and those that get lost.

— Russell Baker

~~~

Assignments

Fiction

Write a story in which several characters are obsessed with, concerned about, and/or desirous of the same object. Sneak in a detail or two from your real life.

Nonfiction/Memoir

Write an essay that uses an object you own, or once owned, to explore an idea that is important to you.

Poetry

Write a poem that uses an object of some kind to explore an idea that is important to you. Tell a secret and tell a lie and never tell anyone which is which.

Challenging Variation for "Delusional" Poets: Make it formal, a sonnet, ode, villanelle, or sestina

Requirements for All

1. In your descriptions, make sure you appeal to all five senses.

2. Refer to something chimerical. You may be humorous.

3. Be very bold. Don't worry about writing really badly.

Challenge for the Delusional

Set your piece in a hardware store, supermarket, factory, office, hospital, dump, or other location where there may be thousands of other objects.

Maybe I'm Mistaken

3rd Annual Shore Thing Writing Getaway — 2015

✦

When I woke up this morning my girlfriend asked me, 'Did you sleep good?' I said 'No, I made a few mistakes.'

— Steven Wright

Experience is simply the name we give our mistakes.

— Oscar Wilde

Never interrupt your enemy when he is making a mistake.

— Napoleon Bonaparte

✦

Assignments

Fiction

Two people–perhaps friends, lovers, or spouses–become divided over a mistake.

Nonfiction/Memoir

Write about a wrong number or another mistake that led to something surprising.

Variation: Write about the biggest mistake you or someone you know ever made.

Poetry

Write a poem under the working title Mistaken Identity. Tell a secret and tell a lie and never tell anyone which is which.

Variation: Write about the biggest mistake you or someone you know ever made.

Requirements for All

1. Include the word "bass," (the fish, the instrument, or the sound) and a word beginning with "pro."

2. Steal language and images from a postcard or two, either from your personal collection, or from our virtual postcard collection at *murphywriting.com/anthology*.

Challenge for the Delusional

Include mention of your birthday, anniversary, or other important date.

Shouldn't Have

24th Annual Winter Poetry & Prose Getaway — 2017

I'll take fifty percent efficiency to get one hundred percent loyalty.
— Samuel Goldwyn

Loyalty to petrified opinion never yet broke a chain or freed a human soul.
— Mark Twain

If God lived on earth, people would break his windows.
— Jewish Proverb

Assignments

In memory of the friend you used to have, the gone lover, the long lost American Dream, Brexit, your hair…

Fiction

Write a story about a character for whom something important has broken, disappeared, or dissolved. Sneak in something autobiographical.

Nonfiction/Memoir

Write an essay about something that broke, disappeared, or dissolved that shouldn't have. Tell the truth, but tell it slant.

Poetry

Write a poem about something that broke, disappeared, or dissolved that shouldn't have. Tell a secret and tell a lie and never tell anyone which is which.

> *Variation*: Address a "Dear John" poem to a celebrity, saint, or historical figure who would probably be unfaithful to you.

Requirements for All

1. Mention the name of a tree and/or a brand of furniture.

2. Adapt one of "Taylor Swift's Best Breakup Lyrics" (See Appendix H).

Challenge for the Delusional

Mention earth, wind, and fire.

Poetry

To the Woman Crying Uncontrollably in the Next Stall

Kim Addonizio

If you ever woke in your dress at 4am ever
closed your legs to someone you loved opened
them for someone you didn't moved against
a pillow in the dark stood miserably on a beach
seaweed clinging to your ankles paid
good money for a bad haircut backed away
from a mirror that wanted to kill you bled
into the back seat for lack of a tampon
if you swam across a river under rain sang
using a dildo for a microphone stayed up
to watch the moon eat the sun entire
ripped out the stitches in your heart
because why not if you think nothing &
no one can / listen I love you joy is coming

In the Stirrups

JoAnn Balingit

—for Adrian on his birthday

Dale Evans slipped into hers to ride
Her horse named Buttermilk. I wonder
If God donned stirrups back in the days
Of darkness on the face of the Earth
Or did He ride the planet bareback? Jeeesus!
I hear praise in the examination room
Next door. The horse on the ceiling poster
Wears a white blaze, a slice like day
Between two nights, an ejaculation
To part the darkness always. Always
For your father I was to be the reins,
The ride, the waves, and too much light
When what I wanted was to be the stony
Brook that gallops to a dark clearing.
You too are a dark clearing. No more
Memorials, I told him that day, not long
Before your dad and I divided. And here
You are. After Buttermilk died, Dale had
His buckskin hide stretched over a plastic
Likeness. May a firmament of stirrups
Brace our beings always toward
What great light the able body makes
Turning green herbs into meat,
Gathering waters unto one place.

Specific Gravity

Deborah Bayer

Once her heart was ballast in her chest,
so sinkingly heavy she couldn't stand.
She slept for as many hours as there
were memories. She couldn't bear

to look at herself, at her bloated face,
her dull eyes. As time went on, she learned
to throw everything, even her marrow,
overboard. Now, as she goes, she seeks

mirrors, sometimes on muddy puddles,
sometimes on cups of tea. The cup's surface
reveals more of the future than the leaves
on the bottom do. Her countertops

are polished marble – black with a white-
veined pattern like the blue veins
on her white hands. She needs constant
reassurance: she is still here, though

a wisp and air-headed, nothing grounded
about her. It won't be a surprise to her
when she floats away, but she hasn't
yet, at least not according to the sliding

glass door at the corner convenience
store. She orders a foamy cappuccino
so she can see her image refracted
into thousands of rainbow spheres.

Her bones are hollow and brittle.
Her eyes are sharp and bright.
She wears a necklace of paper clips
to tether herself to the earth.

Angel

Frank Beltrano

On the day we buried my dad
I was a small boy again in an over-
sized trench coat as grey as the day.
Ruth bought an expensive coffin.
He deserved it, she said.

That night I lay in fetal position
having asked you to make love to me
and having been refused; you were too sad.
I made you cry. I felt ashamed
I had even asked. As I slipped away to sleep

an angel emerged from my taut shoulders.
In the darkness it was light
but not bright. It floated up, ascended,
a young male angel, as I remembered my father,
not exactly glorious, just there and gone.

Ruth says he is still here,
brings her luck at the casino.
She wins five hundred, one thousand, recently
two thousand four hundred dollars but never
a miraculous amount like a million.

Of late I have read
the Tibetan Book of the Dead.
I wonder what would have happened
if you had agreed to make love to me.
The Book of the Dead says

most people can't bear the light,
terrified they turn aside.
They are then shown lesser lights.
They start having sexual fantasies
become disembodied voyeurs around
copulating couples until they are trapped
in a womb and are born again in a human body.

11:00 PM in Price Chopper

Norma Ketzis Bernstock

I stand in **Produce** deciding
between Romaine and Boston
when suddenly the air
comes alive with Meatloaf,
belting out Seger's
Old Time Rock and Roll.
A man in **Cheese** grabs
a woman from **Deli**
who swings her hips
past **Seafood**
where someone
with a clam
in each hand
keeps time.

At **Customer Service**
clerks beat on boxes
with basters
and cashiers
atop the conveyor
clap hands
leaving shoppers
to bag their own.
I grab a long zucchini
and twirling it like a baton,
step rhythmically
out the door,
the parade
behind me.

And up above—
balloons float free:

> *Get Well*

> *Happy Birthday*

> *Bon Voyage*

Dime Store

Jean Bower

In the train to San Francisco my mother cried.

I didn't ask "why" because my four-year-old heart knew
she couldn't answer. We were running away and there was
a frightening "from" feeling to what that said. There's so
much difference between "away from" and "away to."

I didn't ask about my father or about the slamming noises
from their bedroom, his sour smell, or the bullets in the
ceiling, either.

Much later I learned words like "complicit," "commitment,"
"custody," and "divorce." That day, when Aunt Jesse took us
to the station, I concentrated on "ticket," and "suitcase,"
and "hold my hand."

We stayed in the Drift Hotel in a room with a Murphy bed
which I feared, maybe hoped, would clap shut like a
wooden book and close me up where I was made to run in
place, faster, faster. I knew about Alice, but wasn't quite
sure I wanted to know a rabbit taller, later, than I.

My doll's name was Harriett, and my grandmother had
made her coat and mine. Their navy-blue arms held us,
and their buttons were anchors and that was important.
Harriett's hair was bobbed, but solid as her face. Her blue
eyes never slept and I trusted her to watch—for we were
running away.

The buildings went up and up and up, not like where we
were from where all was more child-sized and not by the sea.
There were no gulls where we were from. In the sky we'd left
behind there was no mist and no girls sold violets on the
streets and we didn't eat corn flakes for lunch and dinner.

The bridge sometimes made a shadow—I've since learned
it was a reflection—like a dragon's tail, and stars seemed to
sit in a sky not quite dark.

Not talking, not asking, not knowing—the empty—was always there in San Francisco where there was a kind of "wait" in the air. We waited at stoplights, and libraries; in the park, on streetcars, and for the mail.

But Woolworth's was a destination where waiting was made timeless by all the wonderful things there were to see, by the wishing sensation the hot dog fragrance caused, by the warm wool feel of the dime store air.

I began to believe that I was a girl in a story, like Alice, that I entered a magical land when I went through Woolworth's revolving door, went down the steps, slid my hand along the brass rail to where the doll in the peach dress winked an invitation to take tea from a tiny cup, and the clown with the constant smile looked agreeably distant and the jewels in the glass case with the golden key sparkled like stars in a far sky. The sailboats with tall masts and the train with a circular track waited for someone to signal to begin. All year long they winked and smiled and waited while I grew taller and taller.

Goddess of the Second Hand

Shirley J. Brewer

Once I spent a morning studying a flower.
My neighbors said I disappeared for a year.
I've missed flights, shown up

for Thanksgiving when only bones were left on the plates.
I do see things clearly, take good notes,
remember to wear a watch.

In the 50's—sitting upright in my crib
holding a metal alarm clock—my photo
graced the front page of the Rochester Times-Union.

I remind everyone else to fall back. *This two-year-old
cannot fathom the complexities of time,
but she has time on her hands*, the caption reads.

I live in my own time zone. Jet lag happens most days.
Minutes vanish like river shadows, or men
I almost married. Early is a bird I never met.

My Husband Is Burning

Jin Cordaro

He doesn't seem to know that smoke
is rising from his left hand.
His whole right arm engulfed
in flame continues to hold
his cell phone to his ear until his beard is crackling.
He goes to work like this. He comes home
and parts of him are gone.
Still he is on the phone, now holding it in
the crook of his neck, confirming his weekend job
while his feet are turning to ash.
He goes to fix his mother's garage door,
broken again, and his ear falls off.
Tonight, he tried so hard to hold me
but there was nothing left,
charred socket for a shoulder,
not even a stub for an arm.

Pink

Joe Costal

I knew something was wrong right away.
Your sonogram's green silhouette—
the screen static somehow troubled, shadowy.
I noticed first, the dull glow of your tiny skull,
its line broken, ragged as a shotgun blast.

When I realized you were gone, I grabbed my wife's hand,
but she slapped me away. "What are you talking about?"
she asked, though I suspect she already knew.
My crying was only in my eyes, but her whole body shook.

Your older brothers knew about you,
and together, we prayed. Prayed you'd
be a girl, in that light, silly way kids
wish and call it prayer.

I wore a pink Oxford to work that day.
"I know it's a girl," I told the white waiting
room. With a cheek peck and a belly pat.
Said it like I've said a million other little things.

"This is not about you," the doctors told me
afterward, as did our friends, voices from phones.
"This is not about me," I told myself.
As she screamed to be left alone, I stacked clean towels.

Your vacancy throbbed in her.
Real pain—cramps and blood.
For me you were a ghost, a faint beat
I only heard when the house was finally quiet.

Our bodies, filled with nothing,
chased mourning around till dawn.

Alicia's Stereo: Cornell, 1968

Betsey Cullen

More Malcolm X than MLK, Jr., you strut your stuff,
ignite Baldwin's *Fire Next Time* on your freshman corridor –

dark eyes a burst of flak, stare a stun gun, James Brown's
Say It Loud on full blast, chip on shoulder a boulder.

You would have invented the word Honky if Stokely hadn't.
See this white streak on my inner wrist, you spit. That's where

your great-grandfather raped my great-grandmother. (Fact:
of Fanny Lou Hamer's twenty-two half-brothers and sisters

twenty were slaves sired by rape.) I am your RA, a master
found guilty by skin hue, asked to silence your stereo

during study hours. Words like *Turn the damn thing down*
die before uttered; I leave a note rather than take on

anger like yours, holstered on each hip. *What color
are flesh-colored Band-Aids?* my professor queries,

and my gut twists, eyes survey skin-tone pre-stained
by *Jungle Book* stories and Cadillac-in-the-ghetto jokes.

You quit Cornell. Complicit, boxed in by race, two lives
waffle between grief and relief. And years later

I can still hear your stereo blasting — your voice,
Cassandra-like, speaking truth.

Winter Swim

Barbara Daniels

Over the bay, thousands of snow geese
reel through the half-light. They bark
like dogs in the chop of cold water.
I pull my red cap down over my ears.

Effluence seeps from a factory,
filling the air with steam. Ice
on the oily surface rises, rocks.
I lift my arms and dive into the reeds.

The geese nod at my dripping face,
rusty stains on their necks and heads.
I smell like brine, like rotting salt grass.
My breasts bobble in my soaking clothes.

I'm muddied and addled and blessed
by the water. The dunes wait, deserted,
stalled by a snow fence, resolute slats
weathered to gray. The world can't

be mended. But the sun wheels up
from the water. Silver loses itself
near the shore, spreads in patches
that light each wave from within.

Letter, Address Correction Requested, 1990

MaryLisa DeDomenicis

Linda in five years, I've tried seven times
to reach you. There is something I need
to get back to. I don't know what, or why
hearing your voice may help. I've called
your mother who is out of touch, claims
not to know your last name, mumbles about
how she's lost you to the signature city
of Independence: Philadelphia.
411 can't find you in the 215's.

When last we spoke you were bound
by the hardcover of a story your family
pressed you into. Cradled in my ear
from a distant wire, you said that giving
one's organs away would be nothing,
nothing, compared to delivering
one's baby to another mother.

Since then, more mountain has been carved
to widen the road I drove on to get here
where, sea-struck, even the stars smell like salt.

I pore over the faces I see touring
the beaches I live by and think
everyone comes at least once to consider
throwing themselves in. Some days
my eyes cut through the streets, strain
to find you where you walk — maybe —
with your dark-skinned first-born girl.

I imagine we take a streak of green
afternoon, drink our wine red
by the long white river, compare the colors
we've seen the world turn. I could tell you
I see it blue sometimes, and not
have to tell you why; mention my marriage
put away like a badly written book
I couldn't get through; tell how my family,
slow to change, readjusted their stance,
unlocked the door, and how after seven years,
I went back, on my own power, to the house
I grew up in. I would count for you
(Linda, if only I could)

how many people don't incorporate the color
of my child into the fabric of their lives, and after
calculating the number of years it will take
the world to change we could make guesses at
how dead we'd be by then. Linda, listen:

I want to remember us soft, young, hopeful,
when we didn't know the world better,
when we believed we could bear children,
and take them for walks on an equal ground.
These days I don't know what ground you stand
on or if you can stand it. Should I try for five more years

I might find you. I might not even know
what to say, but I would want to say it. So much
will continue between us. No matter
how separate our ends, we are fixed, one
in the other's story, and I have held
your place. If I could reach you, we might

sit down on our older, harder bones, keep our
cool under the half-shade that divides the world
into sides. Call me. I am living proof
we move under Newton's laws, as are you:
forcibly held down, distantly grounded.
Call me. You will find I am both
the opposite and equal reaction to your action.
I will be climbing hills with my dark son.
I will be in the book.

Love,
MaryLisa

The Grand Opera of Boko Haram

Emari DiGiorgio

after Henry Reed's "Naming of Parts"

Here's where the instruments of torture break into song. Earlier,
an open cargo truck, a skulk of men in sweat-stained fatigues.
And later, we shall have what to do after the rapes. But here, here
the instruments of torture break into song. Doe-eyed girls
in plaits learn algebra on handheld slates, solve for x and y,
     and the instruments of torture break into song.

An eyeless machete rears up on its handle. Its blade
is a Cheshire grin. A chorus line of leggy grenades
palms safeties, upturns jowly Buddha faces,
which implies a compassion they have not got. If we add
zero to any number, we will end up with the same number,
     which implies a stability we have not got.

No gossip's brindle or iron maiden where a pair of scissors
or hot coals will do. And please do not let me see anyone
using his finger. You can convert the girls quite easily,
watch the smallest start to weep. A peddler sells twice
as many pears in the afternoon after letting everyone
     touch any of them using their fingers.

And this you can see is a whip, with a voice for soprano
arias. Hear how the notes turn steel-blue block walls
and concrete slab to calm seas, cloudless sky: we call this
a cappella. Calm seized. Clouds sigh. We must be careful
not to make mistakes when dealing with negative signs:
     they call it Deus ex Machina.

They call it the finale: it is quite easy
when the smallest starts to weep: like the whip,
and the barrel's open mouth, and the blade and burnt house,
which implies a hope we have not got; and the location
of the girls is unknown: halfway between sea and sky,
     they're instruments of torture, broken song.

I Am Silenced for the First Time in Twenty-Four Years

Karen Z Duffy

I'm standing in front of my twelfth-grade students
when one of them blurts

"Wow, Mrs. Duffy! I bet you used to be hot!"

The class is still.

1.
Why Johnny, I say, That is not an appropriate thing
to say. You should not be thinking
along those lines at all.
You are in English class
and I am your teacher.
Now get your mind out of the gutter
and open your book
before I have to escort you to the office.

The class is still.

2.
Actually, Jamaal, you're right. I was hot.
I was so hot, packs of wild dogs followed
me to school every day.
The howling outside the classroom
became quite a problem.
I was so hot, boys begged me
to diagram sentences that had dangling elements,
and read Hamlet over and over again,
especially the parts about Gertrude and her bosom.
You would have died in my class,
I was that hot.

The class is still.

3.
Excuse me, Jason, but what do you mean,
"used to be"?
There is no such thing as "used to be hot."
"Hotness" is a relative term
that refers to a gradually shifting audience
and depends on whom is holding the thermometer.

Do you understand?
The same people who used to think I was hot,
still think I'm hot,
because they have also gotten old.
In addition, there are young men who think I'm hot,
though you might not think they're young
because they need reading glasses
but won't admit it yet
which only increases my hotness in their eyes.
Any questions?

The class is still still.

Where are the interruptions?
Announcements, phone calls, maintenance workers,
insects, new students, sick students, paper airplanes,
snowstorms, lawnmowers, fights.

Look at these kids, I'm thinking.
They know nothing about life.
They are 17.
In June,
they'll be 18.
And next September,
they'll be 17 again,
and sitting in my class.

The digital clock clicks 10:34.

Please turn to Act II sc i, I say.

There's a voice in the back.
"Is this one of those plays where they all die in the end?"

Yes, I say. It is.
Now, who would like to read aloud?

The Date

Stephen Dunn

It was afternoon. Not a hair
of her long blond wig moved
as they cruised in his convertible
the town's back streets and avenues.

At stop signs people could notice
the fixity of her smile. At red lights
a disturbing pallor, something off.
So he knew that to really appear

to have a beautiful companion
he had to hit the open road,
and keep moving
at just the right speed.

Soon they were in the country.
The day was bright, warm.
He wanted to keep driving forever,
never stop, gas up

the way those planes do in mid-air.
Earlier, he had dressed her
in a black, off-the-shoulder Versace,
and for a moment feared

what the overly-stylish must –
that she looked oh-so-close to sad.
But now it was just him and her
in his '96 Camaro, and around them

unjudgmental cows and horses
in the verdant fields.
Everything was as it seemed, and what
could be better than that? He rested

his hand on hers. He told her
what she meant to him, and more.
Under the cover of dark, he finally drove
home, opened for her like a gentleman

the passenger door, carried her in,
removed, then hung up her clothes.
He'd return her to the store window
in the morning. But now how chaste

she looked in her nightgown—
and ahead of him nothing
to look forward to but sleep
and the sweet misery of his dreams.

Reunion

Elizabeth Fonseca

I visited you in Florence. It wasn't
our old apartment, but in a concrete block,
squat, square. Something
felt wrong there.
You told me about your new life: a job in sales,
a girlfriend who lived in the countryside
and drank too much wine. Your smile never met your eyes;
your shoulders sagged.
On the console table, next to your car keys,
a postcard of the Golden Sands.
It stopped my breath a moment. How long past
was our honeymoon? Why
was that there? I wanted
to open a window; it was too dark.
When you stood up,
a sigh unrolled from your body
and coated the walls with sorrow.
I stood to leave. Between us,
the baby that never was.

Poof

Sandy Gingras

My mother wants her head to be frozen
after she dies. I'm against it, but
there's no talking to her. She has a brochure.

On the cover, there's a picture
of a white building with no windows.
I tell her, I go, "I'm never gonna visit you there."

She says, "Fine, fine," the way she does.
She reads me the whole brochure.
She'll be maintained at something-something degrees

until they come up with the technology to defrost
her. Then, she says, "POOF. It'll be like
being microwaved." I go, "Think about

what happens to popcorn." She keeps on reading
about how they'll just fiddle around with her DNA,
and she'll grow a whole new body. I don't get that part.

I go, "What if they can't grow you a body,
and you're stuck being an alive head forever."
She says, "Then you'll have to carry me around."

I knew it. I knew it.

Blunt Cut

Patricia Gray

He loved my hair
when it grew to mid-back
and flapped like a horse's mane
during sex. Whip it, he would say
as we galloped. I was filly;
he was steed. Bit to his mouth,
bridle in hand. Fun but no feeling.
      So I cut it —
my palomino hair — and when
he came round after we split,
a photo of my new love
in an old frame on the desk,
he grinned. Does he ride,
dig in? What a sleaze, I thought,
eager to banish the meadow of me
his thoughts grazed upon.

Thirst

Luray Gross

She counts on the moon
that pours pale milk from its pitcher,
unhurried as a serving girl by a Vermeer window,

not the man with the steel guitar
fingerpicking away the time
before he will take off his shoes
and lay his body
down in their cool-sheeted bed,

not their children grown and gone,
mother buried, father
melancholy still.

She snaps leash to collar,
and they step outside.
Only the dog, she thinks, might understand
how it feels
to drink from the moon's crazed cup.

Hugs No Kisses

Robert Halleck

He ran into her
at the post office.
She gave him a hug.
He asked about her mother and
their son who ignores his emails.
She asked about the dog she'd left him
then told him he needed to marry again.
She gave him another hug.
I loved you, he thought,
more than I showed.
I'm sorry for that.

Whatever Happened to the Cult of the Beloved?

Tony Hoagland

and I wonder if I can begin to revive it
with the image of Kath
lugging clothes downstairs at two A.M.
in a blue plastic laundry basket

with a jug of allergy free detergent. Then her sitting
in the apartment complex laundry room,
with her ziplock bag of quarters
and a copy of *Anna Karenina*,

watching the clothes be interrogated and punished
for the crime of collecting dirt,
while I fall more and more in love with her,
and her unhysterical fidelity

to a program of pragmatic realism
in our apparently post-romantic lives.
Whatever happened to the cult of the beloved?

Maybe it is still alive and well in us—
in the land of rent checks and vaccinations,
stronger reading glasses and suspicious rodent droppings.

It isn't about perfumed notes, or holding hands
or tattoos promising forever.
It's about me grumbling

and carrying the garbage out at night;
and then taking a little can
and oiling the squeaky hinge on the garage

that has been bothering her for years.
And a day or two later,
when the door rolls up and down without a noise,

and she asks, *What's
wrong with the door?*
somebody else will look up from the newspaper

and say, *Nothing.*

They Visit Her Eyes

Peter Krok

The floor listens
       to her white slippers.
Her eyes can't find her hands.
She slips into a place
without an alphabet,
where words no longer spell,
stories no longer connect,
life looks for a mirror.
The oven is lit. The witch at the fire.
We come to bring her back
but the door will not open.
Is there a key?
       Is she drifting
where the tide drags the ones
who cannot find their name? Where grief
waits for those who held her?
       She runs
to the river where there is no river,
schoolyard where no one finds the ball.
"Come back," we call, "Come back."
The crows visit her eyes.
       She turns
and looks away. The blue of her body
screams. The claws of the night
will not let go. The dust falls.
She takes wings.

The Night Jesus Showed Up Late for Dinner

Donald LaBranche

It was the night Jesus showed up late for dinner.
They said he asked for me by name, but I was out
in the peach orchard with a long-handled shovel.

I've seen the snapshot of him resting in the chaise
made of faux leather, longer and wider than he
needs. Young Marie is grinning out from beneath it.

My secret is reserve with the cinnamon
for the cobbler, with a thimble of bourbon
to bake in the right amount of Joie de Vivre.

Jesus himself proclaimed the recipe *divine*.
Then the Napoleon brandy flowed and we argued
about Nietzsche, still in Heaven against his will.

When the children convinced Jesus to tell a tale
I wandered back outside to dig in the orchard.
It was dark and cold, and the stars had nothing to say.

Chair

Dorianne Laux

Oh the thuggish dusk, the newborn dawn, morning
cantilevered over the trees, afternoons doing nothing
again and again, like push-ups. Like watching
a redwood grow: fast and slow at the same time.
Clock ticks: each minute a year in your ear.
The days are filled with such blandishments, nights
brandishing their full blown stars, the decade's
rickety bridges, baskets of magazines open-winged
on the porch, rusted wind vanes pointing north, cows
drowsing in clumps on the hills. Will you ever come back?
Will I welcome you again into this house? There are staircases
sewn to the walls throwing bolts of deckled light.
Let's breathe that air. You could sit in a chair, right here.

A View Onto the Highway

Kyle Laws

First time you visit my studio you tell me
you laid down in a bathtub in Brooklyn,
a razor on the lip of porcelain,
decided not to shave your legs.

You point to the dolls in the chairs.
"Your audience?" you ask.
"But what about the empty chairs?" I counter,
"Just gone out for a smoke?"

The black one, the white one, really caramel,
Gwen made for me. Then she drove up
the off ramp, shot herself.
I knocked on her door until my fist hurt,

worried I was being possessive.
Then I read about her death in the paper.
You put the razor away in a glass cabinet.
Within view, out of reach.

Letter to Myself at Eighty

Marcia LeBeau

I hope you know you're still lovely, with a tongue
that can tie a maraschino cherry stem, then turn
the world cockeyed. Your wrinkled branches
remain for you to dance in the wind. Remember,
on your most ragdoll-of-days, you are holy.

But why am I telling you this? Surely you know
more now than I do. And you would tell me
with your gold fusion sarcasm—take it easy, girl.
Slow down. Enjoy the ride, because it's all
a midafternoon spin with the top down, the sun
spraying you with dynamite.

Remember that day in summer, when your oldest boy
was less than one. The way you lay in the crabgrass,
legs and arms skyward with him resting on your hands
and feet, flying while you hated what your life
had become. But you laughed and laughed
with that creature, both finding your way
in the kingdom. That is how it works. Sucking life
into your bones. What the hummingbirds always knew.

Chump

Bryon MacWilliams

Every joke is only part joke.
I didn't get that, at first — like how
not every part of lover is love.
And bittersweet — the very word.
The guidebook says all parts of
bittersweet are poisonous, even
the star-shaped purple flowers
— albeit "only mildly so."
It's like that time you brought me
to dinner with your ex. I didn't get it
until after the bourguignon.
Last night I waited late for you
even though I didn't want you
to come. Please want to come. Just
don't. My place is a terrible mess.

The Name is the Shape of the Body

Elinor Mattern

The skinny bones of "l" and "i,"
voluptuous flesh of love, Fallopian "f,"
the ample eggs of "o" and "a."

Calligraphy puts on the black dress.
Words and their use.
Bones are the stories of words.

You are the curve. The curlicue. You are
the cry in the beautiful handwriting.
The body English. Body of names.

O Elinor! O Grace!
Your dress hangs on the bones.
Bones move in the dress of the self.

And what if your name
was not your name?
Would you still be the body
in the blue dress of the self?

Time Out For My Father

Shirley McPhillips

Everyone, real or invented, deserves the open destiny of life.
—Grace Paley

A maple leaf stretches
into the autumn air,
leathered with the rough work
of taking in and fending off.

Small bones of cellular sinew
strengthen the lobes — keep them
together, hold them apart.

One stemline pulses a red kindness
to the tips — curled, dewslick.

Specks of rain stain its face
and deepen into blotches of rust
like blood from an old wound.

When my father tires of clinging
to what's left of what he has loved;
when he no longer trusts
in the wisdom of his holy roots,

he will welcome the ruthless rush
of windfall.

Sunrise

Patricia A. Nugent

Colors slice a wedge
through the black curtain
Hesitant to emerge
orange light spreads like taffy
stretched and pulled until
the velvet seam rips open
It seems the end
but is the beginning
They look similar
Why do I anticipate darkness?

Mr. Paramecium

Richard Parisio

Seventh grade was hell for me
all over again, as a novice teacher.

Why can't we have a real science teacher,
asked my nightmare student, *instead*

*of Mr. Paramecium, whose
experiments never work?*

I learned paramecia
swim by beating tiny hairs,

change course when they brush
obstacles. They survive by movement.

But I held fast in that classroom,
became an amoeba, poked pseudopods

into each corner. Surround and engulf
became my strategy. Like Proteus

I took any form I needed, survived
by yielding, changing shape.

The students seemed to notice
how I stretched and flowed

toward and around them. Did they say
to themselves, this strange behavior

must be a form of surrender?
Did one, observing it closely,

in the private petri dish of her heart,
give a name to this strange species

of teacher? Did she guess its secret
was a painful new strain of love?

Close Cut

Kay Peters

They say it will grow.
Like grass, I think, a little care, sun, water.

Wisps litter the floor. Too many
Sorry, I'm running late calls.

Scissors' snick, snick

At the sound of the tone leave your name.

He traced the curve of my throat.
He said *love*.

I don't want to look.

Early Morning

Wanda S. Praisner

Only one deer today. Ears twitch, listening.
Such ordinary ease rising out of night
from an earth into which we seal our dead.

It begins a silent meander
with little purpose to where it's led,
the birdbath and what's fallen from the feeder.

An ease I envy on this day
arrived without bidding,
casting long shadows, nothing as yet black-banded.

I sip coffee, pick at crumb cake,
picture yesterday's dead fawn on Mendham Road—
beside me, my son's empty chair.

La Fantasía

Dorothy Ryan

She is swimming laps
in the pool, her body
moving rhythmically
as her brain counts strokes
one, two, three, breathe
one, two, three, breathe
do not think about him
that hot new lifeguard
the eye candy from Madrid.
She turns at the wall,
resumes her count
uno, dos, tres, breathe
uno, dos, tres, breathe
cuatro, cinco, sex—breathe.

Home Decorating

Christine E. Salvatore

His walls are bare because,
having avoided commitment for so long,
he can't remember the things he likes,
has nothing with which to fill
the empty space. At the mall,
he looks at a painting but realizes
if he buys this lighthouse
isn't he committing to a theme?
Then all of the paintings for all
of the walls will have to be seascapes
or sailing ships and before he knows it
he will be buying decorative compasses
and barometers, his friends and family
will present him with models of local lighthouses
and forty years down the road his eulogy will attest
to his love of the sea, of all things nautical in nature,
and they will put a sailor's prayer on his tombstone.

When Anxiety is The Other Woman

Taylor Carmen Savath

I'm cross-legged on the black and white linoleum.
Holding paint swatches and my too sweet cup of coffee
trying to decide if emerald or envy will better match
the oak kitchen table that will arrive this afternoon.

When she comes
from the bedroom
wearing nothing
but the work shirt
I pressed the night before
tells me you won't need it anyway
that she rode you too hard
that I shouldn't wake you up.

When I don't answer
she's displeased
with how loudly
she's being ignored
pours her coffee
turns to the freezer
looks past the toaster waffles
and last night's leftovers
finding the cake
we saved from the wedding
and cuts herself a piece
to eat cold over the sink.

Grace

David Simpson

Shouldering the forty-pound bag of dog food
from the car to the house, I thought
"This is how much of yourself you've lost."

My wife knew a good deal when she saw it:
sign up with Weightwatchers, forty bucks off, one day only.
"Just an experiment," she said, "that's all it is."

"An experiment," we assured ourselves three years before,
when we moved in together. If we can back in
we can back out, no big deal.
But each day, like the next line of a poem,
gets us in deeper, closer.

On the wooden porch, I shift the dog food
to one hand. I hear her playing the piano,
a Brahms intermezzo she's been working on,
still nowhere near perfect, but beautiful
in the way it fills our home,
beautiful, because of her attention to every note.

Call it grace, or the mind
behind the mind that keeps us stumbling
in the flickering light.

Who's Missing?

J. C. Todd

The babies who didn't make it, your parents, theirs
and theirs. Cousins, good and awful, gerbils, the stray
cat who gave birth in the outdoor grill where your father

refused to char a London broil again. Your childhood
home, a tear-down. A volunteer that grew into
the maple where your daughter learned to climb, buzzed down

to a stump. Irene, her quick-switch crazes for collies,
for gumballs, for swamps. Aunts and uncles, former
spouses, lovers, classmates, the Dutch rabbit you walked,

harnessed, and leashed. And the birds, the one or two
each year who flew into the picture window, and
the answer to the question why was it called picture

when what you saw through it was real. The dogs. A brother
you went missing from — now that's a missing you
don't miss the way you miss your baby sister who

you never saw, yet everything you see is because
of her, her disappearance no one speaks of, that
first and always missing the measure of what's real.

Renovations

Pat Valdata

You say the squeaky wheel pushes up the dust
on the bridge under the bandwagon.
I say, stop mixing metaphors and kiss me.
I say, it's time to unlock the spare room,
time to dump what we don't need anymore.
Here's a roll-off box. Let's toss the times
you didn't say you loved me along with the days
I didn't believe you. Let's shatter each small woe
like sheetrock, chuck the big ones hard
until they clang like cinderblocks against
the steel walls. I say make that dumpster sing.

Let's gut the whole shebang: the tacky popcorn
ceiling that keeps us from admitting the other
may be right, the walls you bump your heart on,
the unforgiving floorboards. Strip it down
to the studs. Pry out even the sulky nails.
I still believe in the carpentry of the soul.
Honey, let's hammer us home.

Mr. Moon

John Wojtowicz

"The moon is following me, mama"
she concludes from the back seat
while kicking her feet as these are
the only extremities that her car
seat allows full range of motion.
The shoulder straps pull tight
against her belly button
securing her like an umbilical cord did
when her mother's stomach was swollen
like the sun, uterus a nucleus,
milk hardened breasts — asteroids in orbit.

She believes the moon is now caught
in her infectious pull as well.
I can't argue its power so I just nod
and smile—the solution to most enigmatic
moments like when people assert:
She has your blue eyes, young man
without knowing they are staring into
different pools or when they exclaim:
What an adorable little family!
as we walk past hands locked in line
never realizing I am but an alien
within a purely maternal solar system.

"Do you think Mr. Moon will come
home with us, John?" I look back,
seeing her as I have always known her,
with blonde hair both uncouth and uncut
and say, "Yes," because somehow
I know he's just another wandering body,
formed somewhere else in this empty
expanse of rock and space, captured
by Earth's gravity, while passing close beside.

Fiction

Sweet Songs Never Last Too Long on Broken Radios

Roberta Clipper

after Kelle Groom's poem "Ode to My Toyota"

"I'm on 90 heading west, and I hear this voice, a woman, singing 'round and round and round.'"

"Joni Mitchell," she said.

"What?"

"'The Circle Game.' Are you driving? Talking on the phone?"

"It wasn't on my phone. Not on any other car's radio either. No one's passed me for, like twenty-minutes. No one on the road but truckers anyway. Besides, the windows are closed. It's cold. That radio's been broke for years. Nothing works in this goddamn car. Then all of a sudden, a voice, a song. I damn near went off the road. I thought it was an angel. But there are no angels. I didn't touch it. For fear it would — you know the song. It's about aging, time. You know I — I had to call you. No one would understand."

"Howie, you sonofabitch. Be careful. You could hurt somebody. Ever thought of that?"

"I swear, I never knew. If I'd known, I'd never've touched you, let alone married you."

"Great. So I was the big mistake."

"No, not you. Or anyone. Soon as I found out, what did I do? What am I doing now?"

"You're running away; and you'd damn well better!"

"I love you. I never meant to hurt you."

"You lied."

"Not about the big stuff."

"Define 'big stuff.'"

"Damn it, Linda. I wish I was a kid again. I wish I'd never taken it out of my pants — you know what I mean. When I was, like, twelve I felt my body pull away from me and leave me like — like that green mold killing off all Alexander Fleming's bacteria. You know that story? I'd've died, we all might've died — of strep throat, like George Washington — if that green mold hadn't appeared in Fleming's petri dish like a miracle and killed off all his bacteria. But viruses, Linda, viruses. When is somebody going to look at a bloodstream like mine and recognize the thing that kills the viruses?"

"Howie," Linda said. "Where are you? *How* are you?"

"Cold. I'm cold. It's cold here. South Dakota. Nothing south about it."

Linda sighed.

Howie groaned. "I don't dare let anybody near me for fear I'll make them feel as miserable as I feel now. And I'm a man who loves being touched. You know that, Linda. You, of all people. That's all it was. God, I miss it. I haven't touched a woman since — and don't ask about the — it's you I miss. I called you, didn't I? Told you about the angel. And now I'm cold, it's dark by four-thirty in the afternoon, and I love you. I'll always love you. I know you don't believe that."

Linda didn't know what to believe. And that was the problem. She didn't know what to believe, so she didn't believe anything, least of all the husband who had lied to her, who had exposed her to a virus that could not be killed, a man so beautiful — long eyelashes, clear blue eyes, chiseled features — her grandmother had said he should have been a girl. She should have known. What did the song say about marrying an ugly woman?

And practice had made him damn near perfect.

She did her best to wish him that final accident, but she couldn't. Instead she wished him a good night — his foot off the accelerator and his hands free. She wished him a strip of rooms off the highway, a hot shower, warm blankets, a ticking heater, and on the television naked dancers working out the rhythms he could never get enough of, rhythms he loved that did not care in the slightest about his soul.

The Dinner Table

Kim Hagerich

"You're wearing the blue shirt I bought you for Christmas," the woman said.
"I am," said the man.
 She picked up a knife and faced the cutting board.
"You're chopping broccoli," he said.
"You're eating a piece of broccoli before we've sat down to dinner."
 His right eyebrow lifted with her intonation.
"I can see heavy clouds outside the window," he said. "The weather report
 said it would rain through tomorrow."
"I think they might cancel the game."
"You can't say that," he said.
"There is that possibility."
"That's true," he said. "Someone had his hand amputated in a botched robbery."
"I heard about that. It was the automatic safety lock. He must not have known."
"You can't get inside his head."
"We're not criminals," she said.
"We might skirt a law or two."
"You can't get inside *my* head."
"I know *I* certainly do."
"When was that?"
"Yesterday. I used the 15-minute-meter for an hour and a half. I didn't even
 have anything to do. I just sat there in my car."
"If a police officer had asked you to move, you would have been obliged to do so."
"I wouldn't argue with that."
"What did you do?"
"I watched several people enter the post office. A woman had a business
 envelope which was a good two inches thick."
"Two inches thick? That's a lot of business."
"It could have been a letter."
"No one writes letters anymore."
"Don't be hyperbolic. That's when I heard about the amputated man."
"I guess you heard the whole story then."
"You guess?"
"The broccoli has brightened and wilted in the steam."
"Which means?"
"You can set the table now."
"Now is the time?"
"You could have set it ten minutes ago with no real difference."
"A bit more dust."
"Are you saying it is dusty?"
"The amount of dust one would expect considering there is always some
 around. A sponge?"

She tossed it to him.

"The napkins are going to stick to the table a bit, but we will still be able to lift them."

"Bit, bit, bit," she said. "We're ready for dinner!"

"Your voice was loud."

"This is our son sitting down."

"To join us."

"You don't know my reasons," said the boy.

"You are here with us," said the man.

"My mind is elsewhere," said the boy.

"Your body is here. That is the assumed meaning of you," said the man.

"I saw this great movie today. I was enthralled!"

The woman jumped.

"Who was in it? Where did it take place?"

She was removing cutlery from a drawer.

"It made me think —"

She could have placed the cutlery on the napkins, but instead she matched each of the boy's syllables with clanging silverware and the heavy thud of vessels.

"I am laying down the napkins," said the woman.

"The napkins have been laid," said the man.

Playfulness

Kim Mary Trotto

Ben tosses me the ball, flips it expertly to the left, where I'm standing. I let it bounce off my bent fingers.

"Hey," a girl, maybe ten, waves from across the sidewalk. "Not the old lady. Over here."

The young man grins as he retrieves the ball. "Try again," he says.

I catch it this time and close my hand around it. There's still magic in these creaky old bones, I think. But what should I do with Ben's red ball? Throw it back to him? Or to the little girl. Or any of the people who've stopped their strolls through the park to watch us.

What if I drop the ball into my purse, take it home on the bus, show it to my husband? "Look," I could say to Larry. "Isn't this the prettiest red ball you ever saw?" To make him a little jealous, I'd add, "A handsome young man named Ben gave it to me."

But Larry wouldn't get jealous. "A stranger gave you a thing and you bring it into the apartment?" he'd say. "Throw that junk away, Zoe."

No, I won't put the ball in my purse. Ben's hand is out and he's smiling big. Such white teeth. I toss the ball up and catch it, toss it and catch it again.

"Young man," I say. "I bet you'd never guess, looking at me now, that I used to work in a circus. Well, I did. Back in the 60s. A little traveling circus."

I send the ball into the air and catch it every time, left hand, right hand, faster and faster. Ben takes another ball from a bucket near his feet and tosses it to me. I catch it, then another, and don't stop juggling. Ben throws one more. Now that's four, going round and round, a blurred red circle above my palms.

Ben is laughing, his big white teeth lighting up the world. "Lady," he says, "you're really something."

The Medrick

Evan Yavne

(Excerpted from the novel-in-progress, *From Away*)

Little was known about what really happened. It was not uncommon for fisherman on the North Atlantic to head out long before first light and not return until well after dark, and most of the boats carried provisions for sleeping. No one knew that either boat was missing until the Coast Guard got a call from the pleasure craft *Daydreamer* that a vessel that appeared to be in trouble was sighted out near the Big Sow just before dark on the second day. As was typical for that time of year, it was an extremely foggy night, with warmer water from the gulf stream clashing with the cold air pouring off the Canadian highlands and out through the Bay of Fundy. There had been no reports of any mayday calls, but there was a cutter out doing training exercises so they dispatched it to investigate.

Coast guard Captain John Langley ordered his radio operator to place an inquiry on all channels to see if any craft were in the vicinity of the famous whirlpool, or if any had heard or placed any distress calls. Trawler *Seabring* responded that there had been a blast of static on channel 16 that lasted for about 40 seconds, but he had assumed it was just his old ship to shore on the fritz again. The lobster boat *Butter'n Work* chimed in that they heard it, too, but didn't think it was anything.

It took close to an hour for the 52' cutter to get to the area where the boat had been sighted, and it followed the strong ping on its radar, scanning the thick fog with its powerful searchlights. When they finally approached it, the heavy wooden sardiner jumped into view out of the dense gray night, tilting hard to the bow, its stern lifting out of the water enough that its full rudder and prop were visible. Other than the reflections from the search beams and the cutter's work lights, the large wooden vessel was dark. The cutter circled the imperiled hulk. Though all hands recognized the boat on sight, Seaman Andrew Lester copied the name "*Medrick*, Eastport, Maine," into the ship's log, and the Captain had his man call in their coordinates and request immediate and substantial backup.

Though it was now 0:30 hours, the chatter on the radio had roused enough of the fishing community that dozens of boats from ports up and down the coast were inbound at all haste, with many others scrambling to make way, running at top speed to aid in the rescue of one of their own. What was, as yet, not known, was that a second boat was already lost.

While Seaman Lester continued, in vain, trying to make radio contact with the *Medrick*, Captain Langley stood by the railing of his cutter calling out to the doomed vessel with a megaphone. It started to rain.

Slowly circling the area, Seaman Miller, manning the light, called down to the captain that the *Medrick* did not appear to be damaged but that she was being pulled down at the bow by a series of docking lines. The rain intensified. The seas were at five feet and building. The Captain announced into the megaphone that the *Medrick* was to be boarded, and into his radio he commanded his men to put on full survival gear and to secure lifelines.

Already anticipating this order, the boarding crew was dressed and on the deck in a matter of minutes. The chop was too rough to risk a direct jump, so an inflatable was lowered into the water and the three-man crew were away.

Pulling up alongside was dicey. The dying *Medrick* was relatively steady in the rising seas due to the weight bearing down on her, but the bounce and slap of the waves had the inflatable jumping up and down alongside, and the men were unable to hold fast lest the ropes cause their small craft to flip over. The only place to secure access was slightly forward of amid-ships, where the gunwale was level with the crests of the waves, due to the weight of whatever was attached to the bow and windless. If the boat suddenly took on water it would capsize and sink in a matter of seconds, taking the three men with her to the bottom with little or no chance of escape. The rain had intensified and the wind out of the north-northeast was up to 20 knots. Visibility was bad and getting worse, and the men had to shout to be heard.

One man stayed with the landing craft, and the other two were tethered with eight feet of line between them as they boarded the boat from the starboard side. The glare of the cutter's lights exaggerated the contrast between shadow and light. They made their way into the wheelhouse. The small room was empty. A few charts and a red thermos had fallen on the wet floor. Shining lights down into the hold, the men could see by the floating debris and gear that the forward berths of the ship were flooding.

Killing their lights to see if any light could be seen coming up from below, the men yelled down into the darkness. Nothing. Turning his flashlight back on, Ensign Richards hollered to his subordinate to secure the far end of the line to a docking hitch and to cut him loose and get the hell out if the shit hit the fan.

"No, Sir," Seaman Michaels hollered back.

"Just fucking do it if you have to, Stan," he yelled up into the light. "If we both die, your wife is going to kill me," he said as he made his way below deck, but his frightened brother-in-law, watching the beam of light working its way out of sight toward the engine room, didn't hear him. He came back up a long minute later shaking his head. "This tub is empty."

The two men stepped back out into the driving rain and fought their way down into the inflatable. Meanwhile, another trawler and a lobsterman were approaching the scene. The *Medrick*, now illuminated on all sides, looked as though she would not hold the surface much longer unless something were done immediately to lighten her up. The three boats had to keep motoring to hold their positions and avoid being driven into each other by the stiffening gale.

Captain Langley could not tell what was dragging the *Medrick* down, but knew that it wasn't the anchors, because they were still strapped in place on the deck. Whatever it was, it was far too heavy. When his radioman called him back to the pilot house, he was handed the radio and told that the lobster boat's captain was on the line.

"This is Captain Langley. Over," he said.

The signal was crackling almost too much to be understood, but the voice on the radio shouted "Hello Captain, this is Bob Singer of the lobster boat *Dora*. Have you seen or heard from the lobster boat *Miller's Retreat*?"

Captain Langley's heart sank at the sound of the name. "Mr. Singer, please repeat. Did you say *Miller's Retreat*? Over."

"Yes, Sir, Walt Miller's boat, *Miller's Retreat*. Most of the lobster pots in this area are his, and his boat was not on the breakwater when I put out. Over."

"Thank you, Mr. Singer. That's a negative," he said, trying to maintain his composure. "We have not, but we'll keep you posted. Over."
Captain Langley turned to his first mate. "Shit, Bill, I got a bad feeling about this. Pull this boat to the port side of that vessel, and put the searchlight down into the water. We've got to find out what the hell's going on here before she goes down."

Pulling up next to the submerged bow of the *Medrick*, Miller positioned the light as instructed. At first the reflection off the choppy surface was blinding, but when he lowered the boom into the water, the light bounced off of what appeared to be a pilot house window, and, like the face of death itself, the gruesome outline of a fully submerged boat came starkly into view. Stunned at first, the men looked up at each other and then stared back down into the water. Petty Officer Stan Michaels read the name out loud. "*Miller's Retreat*, Phillipsport, Maine," was hanging with her stern pointing up, about 12 feet below the surface, attached by two one-inch lines tied to the bow of the *Medrick*. A third line still hung, frayed upon the surface where it had parted under the strain. It was difficult to say how long she'd been under, but it was clear that either the two remaining lines would break under the intense weight, or the looming specter below the waves would take the *Medrick* to the bottom with her.

Seaman Miller went into a full panic at the sight of his uncle's boat. Captain Langley had to act fast. If not for the worsening storm, he would have sent a diver down to look for signs of life in the second boat, but it was far too dangerous. Had she been hanging bow up, it would be possible for someone to be alive in the forward compartment below deck, but, nose down as she was, the areas that might have trapped air would have flooded as soon as she went under. His second instinct was to secure the bottom boat to lines from the cutter, but he feared the rising seas would place his boat and crew in peril, and surely there had been more than enough loss already.

He tried to radio his CO back at the base on the crackling handset, but he was not able to communicate well enough to bring the man up to speed, let alone ask him for orders. He was all alone and he had to make a decision that he knew might not actually get him court marshaled, but would surely haunt him for the rest of his life.

Visibility was bad and getting worse. Langley signaled to his pilothouse to pull the cutter up, portside to the starboard side of the trawler. Pitching as she was alongside the stationary wooden boat, the two-man boarding crew timed their jumps carefully and scrambled back down the deck toward the submerged bow of the *Medrick*, maintaining lifelines as they went. Standing at the rail of the cutter, Langley and his first mate tossed signal markers and lines to the boarding crew, who secured one to the lines holding the drowned lobster boat, and the other to the bow of the *Medrick*. Then they pulled out their knives and, watching for the signal from their captain, cut the lines.

As soon as she was freed of her burden, the *Medrick* bounced up and settled low in the water, gradually righting herself as the water she had taken on leveled out toward her stern. The men paid out line, and dropped her marker buoy in the surf as the shadow of the *Miller's Retreat* slowly vanished into the murky darkness.

The engine room and galley of the *Medrick* were awash, but she appeared sound. The men fought the bouncing seas and gale force winds, and worked wordlessly to secure her, each privately devastated by the image of the ill-fated lobster boat and the horrifying reality that at least two good men were dead. By 01:30 hours, with the winds and surf continuing to build, the steady driving rain punctuated the resolve of the entire crew as they busied themselves with work, avoiding the darkness they all felt. It was far too choppy to do anything but hold tight, hope the *Medrick* held the surface, and ride out the storm in place. It was going to be a long night.

Nonfiction

The Wheat and the Chaff

Leila Crawford

We were having tacos and drinks for my birthday. I ordered something with gin and cucumbers, and the other girls drank wine, as usual.

You've heard the news about the Duggars, right, Carla asked.

Even Mare, the one who didn't know about Caitlyn Jenner for like a month after that "Call Me Cait" cover on *Vanity Fair*, even Mare knew the story that had just hit about Josh Duggar — the eldest boy of a 19 sibling-deep family with its own TV show — that, when he was fourteen, he had molested five girls, most of whom were his own sisters.

And as they shared a bowl of guac and agreed in disgust about the story, my head went perpendicular to Josh: fourteen and life's been all "praise Jesus," and "I love you, Mama," and "say your prayers, Josh," and liturgical swaying, and Christian rock for fun, and a whole shitload of siblings to "keep your eye on for me," and then there's suddenly this pulling, this pulling in his pants. The ache and the delight — that tightness he knew was born of and headed for shame. And it came when he wasn't even thinking of *anything*, seriously nothing at all, and it came when he willed it wouldn't, and it came even though he prayed it wouldn't. He prayed for his siblings, for his parents, for the unfound, for the unborn, and for the sinners, but it didn't work. All it took was one second, ten seconds, and there he was doing it again—to himself, to her, to her, to her, to her, to her. She was so young, and she didn't know anything about this yet, so he made it OK for the moment. Just a moment and he'd be OK again, back in his room and breathing and counting like he liked to do under his reversible comforter, his brother nearby in the next bed, his own pillow still smelling like sweat but cooler now since he had gotten up. God, his pillow smelled good.

Just like that it came: a swelling in the skies, blue turning gray turning smoke gray. Airplanes at first and then none, all cloud cover, all tight humidity — all full, all tense — all needing release, escape, thin air.

If I could scream or shit or explode or gash myself, the sky says, I can be blue again. I can be me again. And so it pours. It poured.

It poured outside the bar where we sat at a high-top though I would have preferred the anonymity of the sticky bar. I wanted to stare at another city's baseball game, at the bottles and the mirrored wall behind them, not at my friends' eyeliner, not at the smooth leather of one's wristlet, not at the other's smudged iPhone screen as she thumbscrolled through pictures of her children to show us.

I feel so sad for him, I said. Mad at his mom and sad for him. It was pretty simple what I said there: sad, mad. And I know I'm all ego and virtue here. I know I'm supposed to admit to not knowing it all. But for fuck's sake, for Christ's sake, I do know *this*. I have deeper waters here. My mind moves in colors, and waves, and all these goddamn tangents. There is never one direction only, girls. Not even one universe. How the fuck could there be just this: bad and good? Shit gets complicated.

But when they asked how I could feel sorry for him when he was the one, the perpetrator, the sicko, the child molester (Jesus Christ it makes me sick, one of them said), I couldn't get the full truth out. They were staring at me with their eyes straight-on, not looking down at menus or phones or black bean sauce congealing on plates or lip gloss marks on wine glasses, so I couldn't even hate on myself for my shitty purse or the fact that I haven't taken my children to Picture People portrait sessions yet like Carla does every goddamn season. I had to look back at them for real, and it was only partially true what I answered.

I'm sad because he tried, I said. He tried. He went to Mom. He told them. Who *tells*? In this sort of situation, who actually tells their parents? But he *did*. And they prayed on it. Of course. And they sought help in a fucking priest. And probably Michelle and Jim Bob whispered late night under matching bedside lamplight about it. There were tears, undoubtedly. They felt sick, undoubtedly. But he told. Isn't that enough? Who *tells*? Who *shows* their shame? And, *and*: he told his future wife! Her parents. Who tells their future in-laws their saddest, most disgusting truth—that his pit has gone rotten, that he's wrong, he's fouled, he's not like them, not like he's supposed to be, not what God had planned for him?

And I'm mad. What kind of mother stops her son's treatment at a visit with a priest and then a family friend? How could she not involve a professional? Christ, save that boy. He's your child. That's your only job: protect your children. Feed and protect your children. Let them live.

But of course I couldn't say any more than that. I'm a judgmental coward. Look at me: I'm so distracted by my own shame that eye contact hurts. I'm pointing fingers all around as I cry for justice. I'm discovering the multiverse and hanging an American flag for Memorial Day. I'm teaching my kid's CCD classes but betting on reincarnation. I'm praying for Josh as his sisters read from the Bible.

They're the most beautiful creatures I can imagine, these sisters. These sisters who are wiser than Mom could ever hope for, who are more gentle, who know how to love. And forgive.

Of course I couldn't be completely honest. Is there even such a thing?

The Track

Frank Finale

The cinder track across the street from the el encircled a grass field and part of my life. I practiced after classes five days a week, four years in all, with the track team at New Utrecht, the same high school my father went to as a boy. When it rained or snowed, I worked out in the long hallways of the school doing wind sprints, which consisted of running down the hallway, jogging back to where we started, and doing it again. One would think such repetitive strides would be boring. But it wasn't. Each one was different and had its own movements that I tried to perfect: speed, length of the stride, pumping of arms, and high knees. Emptied of students, the hallways amplified the slaps and squeaks of our track shoes and the echoing shouts of, "High Knees! High Knees!" The stale air of last lunches and faint scent of wintergreen hung in the hall.

I was grateful, though, when warmer weather arrived. I could go outdoors and run the track again. The track had some give, unlike the hard-surfaced hallways that caused shin-splints. Often during the indoor season when we left the locker room, the odor of sweat and wintergreen lingered. The track became a relief from a full day of classes. Shedding my school clothes, I changed into running shorts, a track shirt with a winged foot on front, and spiked running shoes. Already, I felt lighter. The track was another realm: the fresh air, the crunch of cinders, the spring in my stride, the lean into the turns, and the kick off the last turn, my lungs burning as I lunged towards the finish line.

This had been my father's track. Different coaches; same track. I met my father's coach once. He came back to visit and wanted to take a look at the track team. Barney Hyman, a school legend, whose teams won numerous track championships. The burnished trophies in the showcases that we passed on the way to classes each day testified to this. I spotted the coach walking near the finish line on the track. Swallowing my adolescent anxiety, I went up to him and asked if he remembered my father Ralph Fennelli? "Hmm… Yes, I do. We called him 'Babe.' When he ran the 60 Yard Dash in the armory, his legs were powerful pistons. He'd shake the armory floor," he said. A faint smile broke out on his grizzled face, "They dubbed him 'Babe' when he started for the 880 yard relay team that broke the record."

"Babe Fennelli." I spotted it in the *World Almanac* under high school track records and asked my dad why he changed the name to "Finale." "People had trouble spelling that name." "Oh, I see." It was only much later, when I learned how reluctant employers had been to hire Italians and other immigrants, that I realized why he probably adopted a more familiar spelling.

In spite of the medals I brought home, my father's enthusiasm was tepid at best. When I told him I was chosen Captain of the track team, he responded with, "Nice but what about your studies?" It wasn't until I went to college, left track, and received a medallion for my high grades, that I discovered he was proud of me. I heard it from the people he worked with at the V. A. Hospital in Brooklyn. "Yeah," Pete, his best friend, told me, "he shows that *damn* medallion to everyone, even the doctors."

Years after my father's death, I attended a 50th year high school track reunion. I was amazed to find out from my co-captain Ron that there is no more track team. And, no more track. It's all a grassy field for football players now. The only place that cinder oval exists is in the minds of the former track members who once ran there.

Oh, my father, I remember you best pounding the pavement to catch the last bus to the Staten Island Ferry before it left for Brooklyn. The driver held the door open until my younger brother and I caught up. It was the only race I ever saw you run.

Egged On

Anndee Hochman

I was nineteen, wearing a borrowed black peasant skirt and a blistering sunburn, when I ate an egg for the first time. I'm exaggerating, but only slightly. The peasant skirt — that's true — and also, sadly, the sunburn, which I'd treated by smearing fresh aloe over my pink, puffed cheeks and shoulders.

I *had* eaten eggs before, but not since age two, when my grandfather cracked one into a heap of mashed potatoes, gave it a perfunctory stir with a teaspoon, and proceeded to feed it to me. I remember the swirl of bright yolk and stringy white, the egg pooling and dribbling down the mashed potato mountain, and the gelatinous strands that swayed from the spoon Pop-pop aimed at my mouth.

I gagged once, then clamped my lips shut. My grandfather tried gamely: "C-A-T, cat, R-A-T, rat…up goes the plane and…into the airport" — but I was resolute. I was not going to eat that egg. For seventeen years, I avoided eggs and all their yolky by-products: the ragged yellow border clinging to triangles of French toast, eggs scrambled or fried or — the worst — sunny-side-up, with their quivering yellow eyes and opaque islands of white. I wouldn't eat quiche, or custards, or meringue; even soufflés, poufed on an eggy exhalation, were suspect.

But at nineteen, my skin on fire from hours in the Florida sun, my college roommates cheering me on, I agreed to one tentative bite of a well-cooked mushroom omelette. Max and Pam waited, their forks poised. I cut a small piece, placed it on my tongue and chewed. Salty curds, a bit of foresty sautéed mushroom, a slip of sharp melted cheddar. "It's — um — not bad," I said. I felt a flush of disorientation; maybe it was the sunburn, or maybe something else. Seventeen years is a long time, but the rest of my life was even longer. A world of omelettes and frittatas awaited. What else had I been missing? What else had I been afraid to embrace?

Sammy

Marissa Luca

Your mom had had one drink too many, or she had leaned over to check something in the backseat, or she had looked in the rearview for a minute too long, or there was a tornado that picked up the car and carried it, or a spaceship flew overhead and distracted her. I was never sure what happened — there was beer in the trunk, but my parents didn't want to talk about it. She was fine, and your sister had a few scrapes and bruises.

We weren't sure whether it was your car we saw when we first rode by, my mom driving, her hair blowing in the wind. I looked out and saw the metal strewn across the street, the smoke, the flames, the broken glass scattered on the road. The car had crashed into the woods, was wrapped around one of the trees. The red paint was scratched and chipped, glowing in the sun.

"Is that Sammy's car?" I asked my mom.

She had slowed down the closer we got to the wreck. Her hands clutched the wheel, tight and desperate. She knew the answer before I had asked, and she gave me a smile, the kind that parents give to children when there's something they don't want to explain, and I knew, even as we turned the corner and checked your driveway.

Empty.

The sirens were deafening.

Later, we learned you were paralyzed from the waist down.

I remember watching with you and your sister as your dad built a ramp for the wheelchair in front of the house. We looked at our shadows in the afternoon, cast against the green of the grass, one small, short tot barely out of kindergarten, one short and chubby, and your shadow was sitting, the light shining through the cracks of your wheels.

We used to have races in your backyard, and although you couldn't run anymore, you could scoot faster than some of us could sprint. I watched as your arms became strong, as you lifted yourself in and out of that chair, watched as your hair spread across your bed as your mother changed the diaper that you were now forced to wear. We made jokes about poop and pretended that everything was normal.

No longer did you and I craft finish lines out of old tarps and waving arms; instead, your dad bought a basketball hoop and we only had one ball but we would take turns and I can still smell the rubber and hear the shouts and the encouragements. We could still draw in the streets, messing up our clothes with chalk of all different colors. We could still laugh and joke and be home late, still eat cereal and watch TV and play with Barbies, and in the summer, when it was really hot, you would wear floaties and we would go in your pool and drift aimlessly, staring at the sky.

Maybe you weren't terribly upset about things. You cried, of course, and I remember when you'd throw tantrums and when your mom would yell and your sister would join in, but you never seemed to question why things had happened to you, you of all people, Sammy with the big smile and the fast legs. I cried after finding out that you would be unable to walk, not because it lessened your value or demeaned you but because I could not figure out why you had been involved, why it had to be you, my best friend, and I felt ashamed that I had not been able to take the brunt of it all, that I could not protect you.

One day, though, a few months after the accident, while we were blowing bubbles, I looked up and the sun was shining and the bubbles were pink and your haircut was uneven and you were laughing, your eyes crinkled, and you were so damn happy, with flower stickers on the arms of your wheelchair and I knew that you had known, all along, the secret to it all. Perhaps you had known even before that day when the glass glittered like gold on the pavement: that we cannot change what happens to us, we can only react. You could not go back and tell your mother to stop, to look both ways, or hold her hand instead of watching it wrap around the neck of a bottle. You could not stop her actions, could not write a letter to some divine being asking for a re-do because it would just be returned to the sender. But you could, and you did, love her, fiercely, in that way a child does, and you looked at me with your nose scrunched and asked what are you looking at?

Your ugly face, I said.

You laughed and threw the bubble mixture at me, and it was sticky, and we were a mess by the time the fireflies came out to join us, but we didn't care, because we were young and we knew. We knew, Sammy. And we always will.

Eulogy for a Marriage

Amanda Morris

I walk through the nature preserve looking for a resting place as heat pricks my skin and sweat rises on my forearms and shins. The spot must be just right to honor what we had. A curve in the dirt path, a tall, straight tree with a wide August canopy, a clearing with wildflowers in white and purple, and dark green ferns. This is it. I stop and breathe in the humid weight of the late Alabama summer. I want to be sure. Yes. The perfect spot for a funeral.

I take the bag out of my pocket and remove the object inside. Bands of white and rose gold, nicked and scratched. This ring lived on my left hand for almost ten years until my husband asked for a divorce. The emotional aftermath drove me to hide it in a small box in the back of a drawer. I don't believe in selling such a story-loaded object, nor could I discard it as garbage. For years, I couldn't bring myself to part with it.

After our marriage ended, I earned my Ph.D., landed a tenure-track professor position, and moved back to my home state of Pennsylvania. Still, I feel tied to the past. Standing here with this ring, holding its weight in my hand, I allow myself to feel and remember. I need a ceremony to close this chapter.

"From this day forward"

We started as friends.

I found this written on the Engagement page of our wedding keepsake album:

Date: Tues. June 10 8 pm-ish — in the rain
Place: Yellowstone National Park overlooking Old Faithful at Observation Point

Craig waited till the crowd dispersed and told me to close my eyes. He spoke of all we'd been through, how much he loved me and wanted to spend the rest of his life with me. He placed the ring on my finger—I opened my eyes — he got on his knees in the mud and asked me to marry him.

After many kisses and giant hugs, he picked me up and tried to spin, but his feet locked in the mud and down we both went — inches from giant boulders poking out of the ground. I gashed my hand, he twisted his ankle — we limped, laughed, and cried all the way down to the Snow Lodge.

We love each other completely and are entering marriage with eyes wide open.

What that narrative doesn't tell is that I had delivered an ultimatum. We had been a couple for six years and lived together for two before I bowed to social expectation and family pressure.

We are supposed to marry our best friends. That's what people do, right?

"To love and to cherish"

Further in the keepsake album, a page called The Wedding Day:

Our Wedding Apparel: dark gray pinstripe, double-breasted suit w/black dress shoes, and tan and black tab collar shirt

pale pink long dress w/short sleeves, cream shoes, pearl crown, cream garter — carried prayer book (was Mom's) covered in cream, and white ribbon, and 2 silk roses (cream and pink tips)

Special Moments: Pacing in the undercroft, I was so nervous, and I was shaking from sheer joy and the magnitude of what we were about to do. Walking down the aisle, I saw only him and when we looked into each other's eyes and said our vows, my heart melted. I am his forever. Funny — he tried to put the ring on my index finger twice, but finally got it right!

Looking back, the warning signs were all there. Little moments of doubt, privileging our family's desire to have a traditional small church wedding instead of a destination beach elopement. And the misfire on the ring finger. Twice.

I roll the ring between my fingers and lean my other hand on the rough bark of the tree. The rosy reflections of our wedding keepsake album don't resonate with me today, yet they also don't feel hollow. Those moments happened. Those feelings were real. I just didn't write the whole story because keepsake albums are for romance, not reality.

"For better or for worse"

I was always leaving.

Two months after our nuptials, I left to attend a month-long writer's residency. I had applied the previous year, was accepted, and had no intention of denying myself this opportunity.

I left my new husband with my cat and all the responsibilities of the household and went to Vermont to write a novel. At the time, I had no ill-will toward the man, just a more powerful desire to pursue my professional goals than to stay home in a constant state of frustration.

In response to the long drone of annoying conversations over the simplest of inconveniences, as well as his unwillingness or inability to change, I would leave. Sometimes for a weekend, sometimes a month. Always alone.

To escape.

He wasn't always honest.

We shared an interest in community theatre. He acted in shows that I directed and we had a lot of fun.

One night after rehearsal, Craig showed me a giant gas-station mug:

"You know I take this to every rehearsal, right?"

"Yes," I responded, annoyed.

"Ever wonder what's in it?"

"Water, I assume," I said, yawning.

"I've been filling this with vodka and ice and drinking it throughout the night." His statement was so plain. A cry for attention and help, which I ignored.

We would then fight. A real fight. A screaming, throwing, nasty fight that surely sounded as if we hated each other. And looking back, I wonder if we didn't, a least a little. He felt trapped with his best friend who wasn't paying any attention to his slow downfall and I felt trapped with my best friend who was making all the wrong decisions and making my life hard. Amazing that we lasted so long.

I suspected something about Craig's odd behavior, and I wanted to see how he would react, so I asked, "Did you stop taking your meds?"

He looked me in the eye and said, "No."

I let it go, even though my instincts screamed that he was lying, that his behavioral changes were the result of his stopping his OCD medication, and as his wife, I should push the issue. I didn't. Because I was on deadline. *If he wants to lie to me, fine. I'll just go about my work,* I thought. *It's not my problem.*

I was so wrong. My husband was suffering. As I had learned, people with OCD often stop taking their medication to resist the reality that they need these drugs to function. Looking back, my heart breaks. I did not have the maturity or desire to be the support system he deserved. I took "for better or for worse" and crushed it under my ambition.

Sitting cross-legged on the forest path, I grasp the ring in my clenched fist and mourn for the people we were. We did love each other, but we didn't know how to be a married couple. I feel our failure with every hitched breath I take. Our marriage exhausted us. Still, we renewed our commitment to making it work, and planned for a future together.

"In sickness and in health"

Two days before we were to leave on a Caribbean cruise to celebrate our new beginning, I slipped on black ice at a car wash and shattered my right ankle and fibula, dislocating my foot so completely that it hung off my leg like a piece of meat.

Morphine. Screaming through X-Rays. More morphine.

"This is the worst ankle break I've ever seen," the surgeon said.

Vomiting. Pain. More morphine. Surgery. Pain. More morphine.

"I'm sending you home, but don't touch your foot down at all. Not the tiniest touchdown. If you do, it will shift all the pieces of bone that I put back together and you will never walk normally again."

Craig stepped up.

He helped me up the stairs to our second-floor apartment and onto the couch without one single touchdown of my right foot. He spent the next six weeks getting me food, helping me go to the bathroom, and setting up sponge baths on a chair. He took care of me with all the love, sincerity, and maturity I had always known he possessed.

"To have and to hold"

Once the cast came off, I wanted to have sex. Gently and carefully, we tried. And failed. He said softly, "I see you differently now. Before, you were a rock. Someone who never got hurt, who was never weak. I just can't. I'm sorry. I can't."

No more physical intimacy. This marked the beginning of the end.

The next summer, I attended Indiana University of Pennsylvania's summer Master's program. I moved into a motel room near campus for the summer, a scant two-hour drive from Pittsburgh where Craig remained. We saw each other on weekends, but the distance between us was palpable.

That fall, we moved in together near school. Most of the time, I demanded that he leave me alone so that I could read and study. Whenever he would come into my office and ask one of his well-worn questions, I would respond with aggravation and impatience.

During that first full year as a Master's student, I didn't feel like a married woman. I also didn't feel like a student because most of the others were younger than me by two decades. I didn't feel like a writer because I had stopped writing for myself or for clients. I didn't know *me* anymore. So I got a job working as a grill cook in Yellowstone National Park for the summer.

Again, I left. And Yellowstone was the most healing time for me emotionally, physically, and mentally. But when I returned, it was clear we were on different paths. Craig had begun a second BA so that he could pursue his own advanced degrees, and I spent that autumn putting my applications together for Ph.D. programs across the country.

When I was accepted into Auburn University's program, Craig was excited for me. He drove the moving van down to Alabama and I followed in my car. We had divided our belongings and he helped me load mine into my new apartment. At the airport, we stood at the entrance to the security line chatting about Thanksgiving and this new adventure.

Beneath the cacophony of airline announcements and wheeling luggage, a silence settled between us. Our eyes met and we both teared up. We hugged so hard and tight, wanting the past eight years to have been better, different, more successful.

I watched him walk through security. Then I turned and walked into my future alone, still unwilling to acknowledge that our marriage was over.

Kneeling down in the dirt and moss, I use a stout stick to dig a hole in the soft earth, breathing in the decaying life of the forest. My heart is calm and my spirit feels the release as I bury my wedding ring at the base of a strong tree in the place where I have walked dozens of times during my time in Alabama. This place helped me find myself again.

I stand up, brush off the dirt, and take one last look around, already feeling my past recede and my future clamoring for attention. We survived our marriage and are better for the experience.

As I retrace my steps, I have three distinct thoughts.

We grew up together.
We learned what not to do.
We remain friends.

Story on a Winter Beach

Mimi Schwartz

Spirit is the art of making what's blocked start moving again.
—Rumi

When I was forty-seven and diagnosed with breast cancer, I gathered every good-luck story I could: about my college roommate's mother who had breast cancer thirty-five years before; about my colleague who called to say she'd had a double mastectomy twelve years earlier; about my good friend Sue who had had three cancerous lymph nodes, ten months of chemotherapy, and looked terrific three years later, better than before.

These stories helped me get on with my life as mother, wife, teacher, writer, daughter, and friend. The darker stories of those having problems, of those who didn't make it, felt dangerous, like a jinx. So I stayed away from the breast cancer support groups and avoided articles with titles like "The Anguish of Breast Cancer," and "Victims of Mastectomy." I wanted no anguish, no victimhood — only lucky stories that encouraged me, six weeks after my mastectomy, to say, "I had breast cancer."

Years later, I still say "had." But the further I got from my mastectomy, the more I realized that my old definition of "good," i.e. cancer free, was too limited. It allowed luck to override the power of spirit; and stories of spirit, unconcerned with luck, are the *really* good stories.

I first realized that on the beach of Cape May, walking in mid-January with poet Judy Rowe Michaels. It was two years after my mastectomy, and we were both teaching in the Cape May Writers' Getaway, held every year over the Martin Luther King weekend to lift the winter spirits. The crisp air and frozen sand let us move at a good clip, and I marveled at her energy after a second round of chemotherapy. Yes, it made her sick for a day or two, yes, she had lost her hair, "but I'm fine!" she said and started telling me about the house she'd just bought, her first. It sat on a ridge of the New Jersey's Sourland Mountains northwest of me: a renovated hunting cabin with big windows, a wood-burning stove, and — best yet — a hot tub in a garden off the back porch. So much better than the cramped second floor she and her husband had rented in nearby Hopewell for years, she said: "A health-giving space, something we always wanted, but never got around to buying until now."

Maybe she'd live in it a year, maybe twenty years, maybe a few months. It didn't seem to matter, which is what I loved. She never mentioned luck. She had made her own by buying a mountain house and going daily into its "big bedroom/study with its big view." And all the anger and fear we feel when we discover we might die went into new poems like "No Guarantees," which moved beyond those dark feelings into a life she savored, whatever lay ahead:

...I drink fresh coffee my husband brings in
from the café where I used to write at dawn,
I drink fragrance of white stock and tulips,
the bright, pointy, yellow ones traced in green.
I have washed, combed my dying hairs,
welcomed the nurse changing sheets,
over which the doctors stand disputing.
I count invisible morning stars to find
new statistics, number off flower petals,
I imagine I taste a new drug in the coffee that no one
will yet guarantee, like a moon pit where you might
fall forever or crawl up the other side, gleaming.
We trim the tulips' stems to make them
live a little longer; the coffee's
gone cold. X rays are shadows that grow
in the long afternoons, and where they lead, you follow
into an uncertain twilight, trailing your IV.

I told Judy's story two years later to another writer friend, who had started chemotherapy that fall. "Judy's still in the house," I said, as we walked the beach — again at Cape May — that was soft this year from the warm winter, our feet sinking with each step. Barbara smiled, and I told her that I liked her wig. It gave her a zippy look, a thick, blond, Buster Brown cut, much more dramatic than her fine, wavy chestnut. We talked about needing good stories to survive, and she said the story she most counted on was her own. She'd repeat it whenever she could: how she'd fainted in class, how her students had called 911, how the ER doctors had seen a shadow that meant more than a bad reaction to antibiotics, and, most important, how her skill in storytelling ("I got more precise, and dramatic, with each retelling,") helped to save her. Doctors, nurses, orderlies, and nurses' aides all paid closer attention. She'd gotten better care, she was sure — not to mention a sense of control. "Now I'm fine!" she said cheerfully, leaving cancer behind her. We talked about the power of the verb "had" vs. "has" — and how cancer as past tense makes the future more real. She told me about a friend of hers with breast cancer who had just gotten married. She hadn't even waited for the pathology report. *Why should she?* we both agreed in delight.

I told her of my husband Stu's mantra after our double whammy: "You have to play the hand you are dealt, and play it as well as you can." He'd had a heart attack four days after the doctor discovered my lump and had his angioplasty three days before my mastectomy. We were not yet fifty, and the thought that we could die so early had never crossed our minds. But there it was, our safe world unhinged. So now what? I embraced Stu's attitude, and him, and felt more hopeful.

Which is probably why, ten days after a mastectomy, I decided to hold a Passover Seder. Nothing big: just for Stu, our children, and me. I wasn't religious, didn't even like ritual, but somehow I needed to eat the traditional dishes and sing half-remembered melodies from Seders of my childhood, always led by Uncle Julius, always ending with singing about a hapless goat, bought and eaten: *Had Gadya, Had Gadya.*

I published an essay, "A Night for Haroset" — about this night of celebration when I wanted whoever was up there to be impressed "and see us as solid types, not flaky," agreeing "that we should be around a lot longer, cancer and heart attack notwithstanding." I acknowledged my "Why me?" rage, which intensified every time I had to say, "Thank you, God" again and again, it seemed. And as others praised freedom and escape from Egypt with "May the Merciful One be blessed in heaven and on earth!" I sat silent, thinking: What about the Holocaust? And the children of Somalia? And Mai Lai? And what about me, us? We're good people…

I didn't dwell on the despair of the many nights, looking in the bathroom mirror at my jagged scar. I moved to the pleasures of an evening as sweet as the honeyed apples I had chopped — despite my stitches — buoyed by a continuity beyond our own lives. Passover, itself a bittersweet celebration of survival, made me feel part of a long story that gave me new spirit. I wrote: "Even if the cancer spreads and Stu slumps to the floor tomorrow, we are saying words that have been handed down for three thousand years, and they will be repeated next year, no matter what." I held onto that comfort.

A year or two later I received a note about this essay — from Judy Michaels. She'd read it in Calyx and had been comforted by it. She passed it on:

> *I sent copies off right away to three women friends—two Jewish, one not — all of whom have struggled with frightening health crises in their families. One, my office mate, came over to hug me the day she read it and said, "You always know what I need."*

I realized I'd become as brave as Judy, who'd bought the mountain house, and Barbara's friend, who'd gotten married before reading her pathology report. My story had come full circle, a gift with the power to uplift. No matter that I hadn't felt particularly brave that night and had been fearful on so many others, I had captured three good hours, and it had turned my small steps of risk into full strides of bravery that others joined, as we carried each other along, lucky or not.

Sister-in-Lawhood

Jeanne Sutton

It's December 12, 1972. I call my sister-in-law, just before noon, to tell her she is a widow. Her husband, my brother, is dead. At thirty-three. Same as Christ, but I won't say that to Patsy.

My news will not come as a complete surprise. He'd been comatose since he'd stood at the head of his Thanksgiving table, ready to raise a toast.

My father, a good enough Catholic to have his archbishop's support, and the Vatican's permission, divorced my mother a little over a year ago. At my brother's urging, though — just this side of insistence, sweetened with his inexhaustible stock of snappy one-liners — they were both there. On opposite sides of the table, but there, along with my sister-in-law, and their four children, the youngest not quite two, the oldest not quite ten.

A cerebral aneurysm pitched the glass from my brother's hand, bounced his skull off the hardwood floor, and killed him, though not then and there.

They were all in Delaware. I was in Florida with my husband, a golf pro, and our two preschool daughters. He was playing in a PGA-sanctioned winter mini-tour. I was driving the Mercury station wagon I'd dubbed *"Das Boot"* to that week's country club, herding the girls away from the 18th hole, to keep them from shouting "Daddy! Daddy!" when they saw him.

He finished out of the money that day. We were nearing the next club destination, and my first Thanksgiving dinner in a restaurant. Visions of the Indian pudding I'd have for dessert danced in my head as the man at the HoJo check-in desk handed me a square pink "While you were out" message slip. "Call your father," it read. I stuck it in my purse until after I had the Indian pudding. An avid golfer, he'd be sure to ask me, tactfully, how my husband finished. My answers, so far, were equally tactful variations on no win, no place, no show.

"Hello?" My sister-in-law's voice came as a surprise. She'd never been close to my father; their contact was less than occasional, and always at my brother's house. I worried more than once if she'd overheard dad's snarky imitation of her drawl after he'd had a few.

We weren't close either. She started backing off — and I was happy to let her — within minutes of her first enveloping "We'll always be sisters!" hug. The big chill began that afternoon, after I brought up the Equal Rights Amendment. "Are **all** you northern girls women's libbers?" Patsy asked. I answered with a lengthy explanation of the differences between amendment and movement. Patsy praised me for knowing so much. We went on smiling. The ice went on thickening.

"Patsy? It's me. Jeanne."

"Jeannie." I'd long since given up on getting her to leave off the second syllable. "Let me put your dad on."

We headed north the next day, arriving after the second operation to relieve my brother's cranial pressure was declared unsuccessful and his coma irreversible.

It was a two-hour drive from our New Jersey apartment to his Delaware hospital. I made the trip nearly every night, after I put the girls to bed. Just as well my husband abhorred all things hospital; no sitter needed.

On this last morning I was washing breakfast dishes when something zero-chill shot up my spine, ringing my ears and blurring my vision. The saucer I'd been holding broke in the sink. I left the pieces there, peeled off my rubber gloves, phoned my husband's pro shop.

"I need to go to Delaware. Can you take the girls?" Mercifully, he could.

Halfway there, my vision cleared enough for me to up my speed; my ears still buzzed like faulty appliances, short-circuiting any form of thought. I caromed into the hospital entrance, left the car in a no-parking zone, took the stairs to the fourth floor intensive care two at a time, and pounded on the door until a pair of nurse eyes appeared in its narrow window.

"I'm here to see Mr. Carbonara."

The eyes blinked once. Twice.

"I'm his sister."

Another blink. "Mr. Carbonara is — dying," I heard through the little loudspeaker beside the door. It had the same round holes as a telephone, but these were behind silver mesh.

"I came here from New Jersey. Family can visit anytime!"

"Yes, but —" she started to say.

"But what?" I hissed into the loudspeaker.

"Mr. Carbonara is dying — now."

I became the cliché of a million cartoons: a swirl of stars and exclamation points around me, the hapless creature who's just run full tilt into a tree.

"I know," I begged the eyes. I did, now. It's not strictly against regulations, so she let me in, after I assured her I wouldn't cause any disturbance.

Sisterhood is powerful, but I have no sisters. I only had this brother. I pulled a no-frills metal chair beside his bloated body. Searched his yellowing face, crusted-shut eyes, white-flecked mouth for something. Anything. Too many tubes and wrappings for handholding, but there was his thumb. His hairy-knuckled thumb. The monkey thumb he used to punctuate his "*eee eee eee*" imitations, to my shrieks of delight, when I was little, five maybe, and he was ten.

My whispered "I'm here," "It's okay," and "I love you" became mantras, through the few eternal minutes before the surround of machinery made louder, more urgent noise. Above and beyond his mummy-wrapped skull, the bright white sine waves rippling across the glowing green screen slowed, shrank, stretched flat. The bellows in the see-through box on the rolling cart stopped wheezing open and shut.

Before I could bend to him, a flurry of polite, insistent hands appeared. Green scrubs and white uniforms lifted me away, escorted me to the narrow-windowed door, expressing sincere sympathy as they shut it behind me and drew a curtain with vertical stripes, gray and white, across the glass.

Now, time warps while I wait for my nickels and dimes to drop through the payphone and my sister-in-law to pick up.

"Patsy? It's me."

"Jeannie! Where **ah** you?" Her drawl sounds so remote I wonder where she might be.

"The hospital." I say.

"The hospital? The **hospital**?" She repeats, her voice escalating. "I came away two hours ago." She starts to sob. "Doctors **swore** — they swore they wouldn't tell."

"They didn't, Patsy. I — I had this feeling. I had to come."

The silence shouts, until she screams "You *hadda* come! 'Course you did. 'Course you would."

"Patsy, please, I'm sorry." Silence again.

"Don't you sorry me, missy." Her whisper is scarier than her scream. "Know it all. High and mighty. Couldn't just let it be, could you? 'Course not!" The line goes dead. I double over, nauseous, stand up when I realize what must have happened.

Two hours ago, my sister-in-law gave her consent to taking her husband off life support. Years from now fixed guidelines and standard procedures will prevent such unspeakable decisions from being carried out in haste and secrecy. But in this moment, they don't exist. Nor do we know about, or have access to, the new CAT scan technology that would have diagnosed and saved him.

I set the receiver back in its aluminum cradle. Poor Patsy, poor widow, poor woman. Can I comfort her? The wall of her resentment—of what? My going beyond a high school education? Using birth control? Women's libbing? —is so high, so thick, so overgrown … I'll try anyway. *'Course I will.*

Appendices

Appendix A

Some Words that are Hiding in Other Words

ace in bracelet	cute in execute	inner in dinner
age in language	eat in leather	ion in optional
all in alloy	enter in center	ire in wire
anal in analysis	fact in factory	lab in labor
anger in dangerous	flat in inflation	lack in black
ant in want	fun in dysfunctional	lady in malady
ape in paper	fur in furtive	lamb in lambast
arc in larceny	gas in orgasm	lame in lament
ark in sparkle	germ in germane	laughter in slaughter
arm in charm	gin in engineer	leg in illegal
ass in glass	grin in grind	lend in blender
ass in passion	ham in shampoo	lever in clever
bee in beef	hard in orchard	lick in slick
bee in beer	harm in pharmacy	lie in believe
bit in exhibitionist	heat in theater	list in listen
boa in board	his in whisper	live in delivery
bra in vibrate	hit in shit	log in kilogram
car in scary	hit in white	loss in glossary
cast in sarcastic	hop in shop	love in slovenly
cat in catholic	hot in photocopy	lust in illustrate
chic in psychic	ice in license	lust in lackluster
city in paucity	icky in picky/tricky	mental in fundamentalist
crib in scribble	id in provide	meow in homeowner
cry in crystal	if in life	nature in signature
cue in rescue	ink in think	net in magnetic

numb in number

nun in pronunciation

oar in hoarse

one in money

or in horse

ouch in touch

ought in drought

out in couth

over in recovery

pant in pants

pet in carpet

pit in palpitate

pit in spite

rage in courage

rage in garage

rake in brake

ram in frame

rap in rape

rat in fraternity

ration in inspiration

rest in forest

rest in restaurant

retch in stretch

rim in crimson

rod in rodeo

rope in Europe

rot in protein

rote in protection

rough in drought

rum in rummage

rust in thrust

rut in truth

sad in saddle

sage in passage

scent in ascent

sigh in sight

sin in business

sin in easiness

sole in obsolete

son in mason

spit in spite

sport in transportation

star in startle

stud in student

sue in issue

tag in heritage

tap in metaphor

tar in starve

tart in start

team in steam

test in protestant

text in texture

the rapist in therapist

tip in multiply

tome in customer

tong in tongue

top in utopia

tot in asymptote

tray in betrayal

trip in strip

tuna in fortunate

turn in turnip

urge in splurge

vat in activate

very in everything

wage in sewage

win in swing

wish in Jewish

Appendix B
Fortune Cookie Fortunes

Stop searching forever. Happiness is right next to you.

You are going to be hungry soon. Order take-out now.

God has given you one face and you make yourself another.

Do not confuse what is valuable with what is sought after.

The time to settle your mind about relationships is never.

You will be attracted to an older, more experienced person!

You will soon be crossing the great waters.

Don't forget that your roots need watering.

Give a kiss to the person who sits next to you.

Alas! The onion you are eating is someone else's water lily.

The scars of the past will soon be soothed by a passionate new love.

Something you recently heard will be unexpectedly useful.

You will have gold pieces by the bushel.

Nothing is beyond all repair.

Many a false step is made by standing still.

Flattery will go far tonight.

You have an unusual equipment for success, use it properly.

Probe more deeply—there is something you are not being told.

The mood is right for a friendly chat to lead to romance.

How can you have a beautiful ending without making beautiful mistakes?

The only rose without a thorn is friendship.

He who laughs last did not get the joke.

Someone will invite you to a Karaoke party.

As soon as you feel too old to do a thing, do it.

Water can not only keep a ship afloat, but can sink it.

You will become a great philanthropist in your later years.

Others find your life exciting.

If at first you don't succeed—redefine success!

The longer road may have superior scenery.

Initiate a new project in the love department.

Do not cling to any single identity.

How you look depends on where you go.

Your love of gardening will take on new meaning in your life.

Sometimes the common is more valuable than the rare.

The truth touches everyone.

The love of your life will appear in front of you unexpectedly!

The sage is cautious—even when alone.

Your dreams reveal important truths.

Everything has beauty but not everyone sees it.

Some important truths will always remain hidden.

We will not know the worth of water till the well is dry.

Everyone is the architect of his own fortune.

Appendix C
Random Word List

sparrows

legs

names

eyelids

Venus

shells

apartment

miles

ragdoll

Darwin

kingdom

gunmetal

Fido

paper

tongue

sprinted

midafternoon

Galileo

sucking

Gilgamesh

branches

marmalade

stairs

wrinkle

Devil

mask

phone number

novels

girdles

boil

Appendix D

A Selection of Words added to the Online Oxford English Dictionary in 2013 (OED.com)

aquafarm	gambling cock loft	ohmigosh
audience chamber	gametoblast	ooh-wee
audience-friendly	gang girl	orgasmatron
backdated	gangling	overstaffed
bag woman	grey zone	peakman
before-ganger	gurrier	primost
before-tax	ham steak	right of appearance
blue antelope	handy-dandy	right of audience
blue giant	head fuck	serial adulterer
boccia	herb of Paraguay	serial comma
braggadocious	heredito-syphilitic	sheself
brown rat	heself	smart apple
buzzworthy	hims	Smarties
campsite	hoki	steelily
clunker	iron bomb	switch plate
common loon	knobhead	they-all
control group	kombucha	theyself
cred	looder	trixie
credit event	low-lifer	undubbed
defriend	low-maintenance	unlovableness
embryopathy	low-rate	uplink
fire-smarting	meal offering	volcano-seismic
friend zone	misclaim	weself
friendly bacteria	misdelivered	whip-smart
functionality	museographic	

Appendix E
Life-Changing Inventions that were Created by Mistake

The Slinky
Inventor: Richard Jones, a naval engineer

> What he was trying to make: A meter designed to monitor power on naval battleships.

> How it was created: Jones was working with tension springs when one of them fell to the ground. The spring kept bouncing from place to place after it hit the ground, and the slinky was born.

Penicillin
Inventor: Sir Alexander Fleming, a scientist

> What he was trying to make: Ironically, Fleming was searching for a "wonder drug" that could cure diseases. However, it wasn't until Fleming threw away his experiments that he found what he was looking for.

> How it was created: Fleming noticed that a contaminated Petri dish he had discarded contained a mold that was dissolving all the bacteria around it. When he grew the mold by itself, he learned that it contained a powerful antibiotic, penicillin.

Chocolate chip cookies
Inventor: Ruth Wakefield, Owner of the Toll House Inn

> What she was trying to make: Regular chocolate cookies.

> How it was created: While mixing a batch of cookies, Wakefield discovered she was out of baker's chocolate. As a substitute she broke sweetened chocolate into small pieces and added them to the cookie dough. She expected the chocolate to melt, making chocolate cookies, but the little bits stuck.

Potato chips
Inventor: George Crum, a chef at the Carey Moon Lake House in Saratoga Springs

> What he was trying to make: A plate of fried potato.

> How it was created: One day a customer sent back his plate of potatoes many times and kept asking for them to be more fried and thinner. Crum lost his temper, sliced the potatoes insanely thin, and fried them until they were hard as a rock. To the chef's surprise, the customer loved them and wanted more!

The Pacemaker
Inventor: John Hopps, an electrical engineer

> What he was trying to make: Hopps was conducting research on hypothermia and was trying to use radio frequency heating to restore body temperature.

> How it was created: During his experiment he realized if a heart stopped beating due to cooling, it could be started again by artificial stimulation. This realization led to the pacemaker.

Ink-Jet printers
Inventor: A Canon engineer

> How it was created: After resting his hot iron on his pen by accident, ink was ejected from the pens point a few moments later. This principle led to the creation of the inkjet printer.

Microwave ovens
Inventor: Percy Spencer, an engineer with the Raytheon Corporation

> What he was trying to make: The engineer was conducting a radar-related research project with a new vacuum tube.

> How it was created: Spencer realized that the candy bar in his pocket began to melt during his experiments. He then put popcorn into the machine, and when it started to pop, he knew he had a revolutionary device on his hands.

Saccharin
Inventor: Constantine Fahlberg, a researcher at Johns Hopkins University

> What he was trying to make: Fahlberg was investigating the oxidation of o-toluenesulfonamide, whatever that means!

> How it was created: Fahlberg's discovery happened because he forgot to wash his hands. He had spilled a chemical on his hands in the lab that caused his bread to taste very sweet. The researcher immediately requested a patent and mass-produced his product.

Corn Flakes
Inventor: The Kellogg brothers, John and Will

> What they were trying to make: A pot of boiled grain.

> How it was created: The brothers accidentally left a pot of boiled grain on the stove for several days. The mixture turned moldy but the product that emerged was dry and thick. Through experimentation they eliminated the mold part and created corn flakes.

LSD as a drug
Inventor: Albert Hofmann, a chemist

What he was trying to make: He was researching lysergic acid derivatives in a laboratory in Basel, Switzerland.

How it was created: Hofmann unintentionally swallowed a small amount of LSD while researching its properties and had the first acid trip in history.

Post-it notes
Inventor: Spencer Silver, a researcher in 3M Laboratories

What he was trying to make: A strong adhesive.

How it was created: While working away, Silver created an adhesive that was actually weaker than what already existed. It stuck to objects but could be pulled off easily without leaving a mark. Years later, a colleague spread the substance on little pieces of paper to mark his place in his choir hymn book, and the idea was born.

X-Rays
Inventor: Wilhem Roentgen, an eccentric physicist

What he was trying to make: He was interested in investigating the properties of cathodic ray tubes.

How it was created: When shining light through the tubes he noted fluorescent papers in his lab were illuminated even though his machine had an opaque cover.

Appendix F
Sentiment versus Sentimentality

In sentiment, the writer allows you to come to your own feelings by experiencing them along with a character or speaker. There is a sense of arriving at feelings in the present, as events, both external and internal, unfold. In sentimentality, conversely, you get a digested version of what you are expected or supposed to feel. The writer relies on clichés, hackneyed subject matter (beware of puppies and kittens), and an abundance of adjectives to manipulate you into feeling a certain way.

If you went to an art museum with Sentiment, she might lead you to certain paintings. (After all, part of the creative process is selection.) She might even draw your attention to a particular detail, but wordlessly, with her eyes. What she wouldn't do, since she is not Sentimentality, is tug at your sleeve and say things like, "isn't that the most beautiful thing you've ever seen?" or "that's so sad, isn't it?"

John Irving warns us not to banish sentiment from our writing, however, for fear of crossing into sentimentality. In his essay, "In Defense of Sentimentality," he writes: "… to the modern reader, too often when a writer risks being sentimental, the writer is already guilty. But as a writer it is cowardly to so fear sentimentality that one avoids it altogether. It is typical—and forgivable—among student writers to avoid being mush-minded by simply refusing to write about people, or by refusing to subject characters to emotional extremes. A short story about a four-course meal from the point of view of a fork will never be sentimental; it may never matter very much to us, either."

–Daniel Simpson

Appendix G

Maryland Facts and Trivia

Havre de Grace is known as the decoy capital of the world.

Babe Ruth, the Sultan of Swat, was born in Baltimore and attended Saint Mary's Industrial School.

Maryland was the first state to enact Workmen's compensation laws in 1902.

In 1975, Elizabeth Ann Bayley Seton of Emmitsburg was canonized, becoming the first native-born American to be so honored. Saint Elizabeth Ann formed the religious community the Sisters of Charity.

The United States Naval Academy was founded on October 10, 1845 at Annapolis.

Notable African Americans who were born or made their mark in Baltimore include Frederick Douglass, Thurgood Marshall, Howard Rollins, Billie Holiday, Cab Calloway, Chick Webb, Ira Aldridge. Eubie Blake, Jada Pinkett-Smith, Toni Braxton, and Kweisi Mfume

Located in the Chesapeake Bay, Smith Island is Maryland's only inhabited off-shore island.

Ezra Cornell, founder of Cornell University, lived in Bladensburg and is said to have invented the telegraph pole.

During revolutionary times, Rockville was known as Hungerford's Tavern the name of its most familiar landmark. One of the first calls to freedom from British rule was heard at the tavern in 1774.

Channel 67 broadcast the state's first public television programs on October 5, 1969.

When Edgar Allen Poe was originally buried in 1849, it was in an unmarked grave overgrown with weeds.

The Basilica of the Assumption of the Blessed Virgin Mary is considered a masterpiece and one of the finest 19th century buildings in the world. The basilica is the first cathedral in the United States. Baltimore represents the first Roman Catholic diocese.

The first dental school in the United States opened at the University of Maryland.

Samuel F.B. Morse reportedly received the first telegraph message in Bladensburg, in 1844, before his famous "What Hath God Wrought" message between Baltimore and Washington. His telegraph wire had been strung along the railroad right of way.

King Williams School opened in 1696. It was the first school in the United States.

Francis Scott Key, a Maryland lawyer, wrote America's national anthem. It is believed Key wrote the anthem on September 14, 1814 while watching the bombardment of Fort McHenry in Baltimore Harbor.

Chincoteagues are famous ponies from Assateague Island.

On June 24,1784, in Baltimore, 13-year old Edward Warren went airborne in the first successful manned balloon launch in the United States.

Maryland gave up some of its land to form Washington D.C.

Annapolis was known as the Athens of America during the seventeenth century and once served as the capital of the United States.

In 1830, the Baltimore & Ohio Railroad Company built the first railroad station in Baltimore.

The highest point in Maryland is 3,360 feet above sea level on Backbone Mountain in Garrett County. The absolute lowest point in Maryland is a depression, often called Bloody Point Hole, 174 feet below sea level. The area is located approximately 1 mile west-southwest of the southern tip of Kent Island in Queen Anne's County.

Appendix H
Taylor Swift's Best Breakup Lyrics

"The monsters turned out to be just trees" — *Out of the Woods*

"Something keeps me holding on to nothing" — *Haunted*

"It rains when you're here and it rains when you're gone" — *Forever & Always*

"I forget about you long enough to forget why I needed to" — *All Too Well*

"You give me everything and nothing" — *I Wish You Would*

"You can't see me wanting you the way you want her" — *Invisible*

"This is looking like a contest of who can act like they care less" — *The Story of Us*

"Time is taking its sweet time erasing you" — *Sad Beautiful Tragic*

"I lived in your chess game, but you changed the rules every day" — *Dear John*

"I don't know how to be something you miss" — *Last Kiss*

"If this was a movie, you'd be here by now" — *If This Was a Movie*

"I hope you know that every time I don't, I almost do" — *I Almost Do*

"I guess you didn't care, and I guess I liked that" — *I Knew You Were Trouble*

"I start a fight 'cause I need to feel something" — *Cold As You*

"You've got your demons, and darling, they all look like me" — *Sad Beautiful Tragic*

"We're a crooked love in a straight line down" — *I Wish You Would*

"In the end, in Wonderland we both went mad" — *Wonderland*

"The story of us looks a lot like a tragedy now" — *The Story of Us*

"Coming back around here would be bad for your health" — *Picture to Burn*

"You could write a book on how to ruin someone's perfect day" — *Tell Me Why*

"I should have slept with one eye open at night" — *Wonderland*

"Band-aids don't fix bullet holes" — *Bad Blood*

"Just because you're clean don't mean you don't miss it" — *Clean*

"I'm shining like fireworks over your sad, empty town" — *Dear John*

"There's nothing stopping me from going out with all of your best friends" — *Picture to Burn*

Contributors' Notes

Kim Addonizio's latest books are a memoir, *Bukowski in a Sundress: Confessions from a Writing Life* (Penguin), and a poetry collection, *Mortal Trash* (W.W. Norton). She is also the author of two novels and two books on writing poetry. She lives in Oakland, CA and is online at kimaddonizio.com.

JoAnn Balingit grew up in Florida and lives in Delaware where she served as poet laureate from 2008 to 2015. She's author of *Words for House Story* (WordTech, 2013) and was a 2017 VONA/Voices resident in prose, working on a memoir. Latest poems appear at *The Rumpus, Vallum Contemporary Poetry*, poets.org, and joannbalingit.org.

Deborah Bayer's poems have appeared in *Hospital Drive, Mead: The Magazine of Literature & Libations, Serving House Journal, Shot Glass Journal,* and *Petrichor Machine*. She works as a physician in the HIV clinic in Atlantic City, NJ, and she is currently working on a memoir about recovery from burnout.

Frank Beltrano writes every day in London, Ontario, Canada. Sometimes poems come out of this practice, and many of these have been published. In 2011, he came to the Getaway to look for America. He learned a lot, made friends, and is honored to be published here with some of them.

Norma Ketzis Bernstock is a member of the Upper Delaware Writers Collective and the Writers Roundtable. Her poetry has appeared in *Connecticut River Review, Paterson Literary Review, Exit 13, Edison Review,* and several anthologies. Her poems have been honored by the Allen Ginsberg Poetry Awards.

Jean Bower was born in Denver, Colorado in 1933. She is more or less a life-long resident of Colorado, having raised her family of three boys in Montrose, Colorado where she and her husband taught and eventually retired. She has published two books, one of poetry and one of short stories in Spanish.

Shirley J. Brewer graduated from careers in bartending, palm-reading, and speech therapy. Her poems garnish *Barrow Street, Poetry East, Slant, Gargoyle, Comstock Review,* and many other journals. Shirley's books include *A Little Breast Music, After Words,* and — new in 2017 — *Bistro in Another Realm*.

Roberta Clipper teaches at Rider University and at the Winter Poetry and Prose Getaway. Under the name Robbie Clipper Sethi she's published stories, poetry, and two novels: *Fifty-Fifty* and *The Bride Wore Red*. Awards include National Endowment for the Arts and New Jersey State Council on the Arts fellowships.

Jin Cordaro received her MFA in creative writing from Fairleigh Dickinson University. She is a Pushcart Prize nominee, and the recipient of the 2009 Editor's Prize from *Apple Valley Review*. Her work has also appeared in *Faultline, A Smartish Pace, Sugar House Review, Main Street Rag*, and *Cider Press Review*.

Joe Costal lives at the Jersey Shore where he teaches writing at Stockton University. He was honored to be a 2017 Grub Street Boston Muse & Marketplace Visiting Writer fellow. His work has most recently appeared in *The Maine Review, Ponder Review*, and *Pif Magazine*.

Leila Crawford lives and teaches in New Jersey. She studied Spanish, creative writing, and studio arts in college and is proud to say that they remain her three favorite subjects. If she could do it again, she'd add geology and algebra.

Betsey Cullen hails from Pennsylvania and teaches poetry at the Osher Lifelong Learning Institute at the University of Delaware. Diane Lockward's *Crafty Poet II* and Pennsylvania Poetry Society's *Prize Poems, 2017* include her poems. In 2015 her collection, *Our Place in Line*, won the Tiger's Eye Press Chapbook Competition.

Barbara Daniels' *Rose Fever* was published by WordTech Press and her chapbooks *Moon Kitchen, Black Sails*, and *Quinn & Marie* by Casa de Cinco Hermanas Press. She received three Individual Artist Fellowships from the New Jersey State Council on the Arts and earned an MFA in poetry at Vermont College.

MaryLisa DeDomenicis is a Pushcart nominee and holds a BA in Humanities. A recipient of the Toni Brown Memorial Scholarship award, her latest poems appear in *Bared: Contemporary Poetry and Art on Bras and Breasts*, and *Rabbit Ears* (NYQ Books). She is a member of the South Jersey Poetry Collective.

Emari DiGiorgio is the author of *Girl Torpedo* (Agape, 2018), the winner of the 2017 Numinous Orison, Luminous Origin Literary Award, and *The Things a Body Might Become* (Five Oaks Press, 2017). She teaches at Stockton University and hosts World Above in Atlantic City, NJ. Read more of her work at emaridigiorgio.com.

Karen Z Duffy has won writing fellowships from the New Jersey State Council on the Arts and The Norman Mailer Writers Colony. Her chapbook, *Giving in to the Smoke* received the Starting Gate Award from Finishing Line Press. Karen's poem, "World Series, Game 5" was featured on The *NewsHour* With Jim Lehrer.

Stephen Dunn's most recent book is *Whereas* (Norton, 2017). Among his many awards are the Pulitzer Prize for *Different Hours*, and Fellowships from the Guggenheim and Rockefeller Foundations. He lives with his wife Barbara Hurd in Frostburg, Maryland. And the editors of this anthology met in his class!

Frank Finale is the author of *To The Shore Once More, Volumes I-III*. He co-edited two poetry anthologies: *Under a Gull's Wing* and *The Poets of New Jersey* and was poetry editor for *the new renaissance*. He is an essayist for Jersey Shore Publications magazines and has written three children's books: *A Gull's Story 1-3*. www.frankfinale.com.

Elizabeth Fonseca is an avid traveler who has lived in Italy, Turkey, and the United Arab Emirates, among other countries. Her forthcoming chapbook, *This World*, reflects on those experiences and other traveling encounters and adventures.

Sandy Gingras is the author/illustrator of 25 gift books, a chapbook, *Not Even Close to What She Planned On*, and a murder mystery, *Swamped*. She won the Debut Dagger award from the Crime Writer's Association in 2012. Sandy lives on Long Beach Island and owns two retail stores.

Patricia Gray's poems appeared most recently in *Salamander*, in *Tiger's Eye* accompanied by an author interview, and on a poster in selected Arlington Virginia buses for the Moving Words project. She formerly headed the Library of Congress Poetry and Literature Center. Her collection *Rupture* is from Red Hen Press.

Luray Gross, a storyteller as well as a poet, is the author of three collections of poetry, most recently *The Perfection of Zeros*, published by Word Tech. She lives in Bucks County, PA, a few miles from the dairy farm where she grew up.

Kim Hagerich is a writer, English teacher, and intermittent bookmaker. Her writing has appeared in *NANO Fiction, CutBank, Invisible Ear,* and *KYSO Flash*. She used to live in Madison, and now she doesn't.

Robert Halleck is a retired banker living in Del Mar, California with his muse, Della Janis. He fills his days with poetry, hospice volunteering, golf, and autocross racing. He has published three volumes of his poems. Recent poems have appeared in *San Diego Poetry Annual, Paterson Literary Review*, and *The Galway Review*.

Tony Hoagland's *Application for Release from the Dream* was published by Graywolf Press in 2015. He is working on a craft book about poetry called *Five Powers, Forty Lessons*. He has a collection of poems forthcoming: *Priest Turned Therapist Treats Fear of God* in 2018. He lives in Santa Fe, NM.

Anndee Hochman's column, "The Parent Trip," appears weekly in *The Philadelphia Inquirer*; her commentaries, personal essays, and reviews appear regularly in *Broad Street Review, Purple Clover*, and *Newsworks/ Speak Easy*. She is the author of *Anatomies: A Novella and Stories* and *Everyday Acts & Small Subversions: Women Reinventing Family, Community and Home*.

Peter Krok is the Humanities Director of Manayunk Roxborough Art Center since 1990; Editor-in-Chief of the *Schuylkill Valley Journal* (SVJ) founded in 1990, and SVJ Online at svjlit.com. He is known as the "red brick poet" because of his connection to Philadelphia. His book, *Looking For An Eye*, was published in 2008.

Donald LaBranche's practice includes poetry, T'ai Chi, occasional teaching at Quaker Meeting, as well as wide-ranging conversations about show tunes with his granddaughter. His most recent chapbook, *Composed of Diamonds and the Ecstasy of Light*, was published by Casa de Cinco Hermanas Press.

Dorianne Laux's most recent collections are *The Book of Men*, winner of the Paterson Poetry Prize, and *Facts about the Moon*, winner of the Oregon Book Award. Her *New and Selected Poems: Only As The Day Is Long* is forthcoming from W.W. Norton. She teaches poetry in the MFA Program at North Carolina State University and is founding faculty at Pacific University's Low Residency MFA Program.

Kyle Laws is based out of the Arts Alliance Studios Community in Pueblo, CO. Her most recent collection is *This Town: Poems of Correspondence*, written with Jared Smith (Liquid Light Press, 2017). She is the editor and publisher of Casa de Cinco Hermanas Press.

Marcia LeBeau's poems have been published in *Painted Bride Quarterly, Rattle, Moon City Review, SLANT*, and elsewhere. She holds an MFA in poetry from the Vermont College of Fine Arts. Together with her husband, she co-founded The Rectangle Studio & Gallery in Orange, NJ. marcialebeau.com.

Marissa Luca is currently studying literature and communications at Stockton University. A semifinalist for the 2013-2014 Eichner Awards, she is a Staff Writer at the *Argo*, a newspaper affiliated with Stockton, and Vice President of the Literature Club. When she isn't writing, she's with her family and friends, or playing video games.

Bryon MacWilliams' work has appeared in publications big and small, including *The Literary Review, The New York Times, The Chronicle of Higher Education, Nature*, and *Science*. He is a translator of Russian literature into English, and his memoir, *With Light Steam*, was published in 2014 by Northern Illinois University Press.

Elinor Mattern's poems and non-fiction have appeared in *Washington Square* and *The Philadelphia Inquirer*, among other publications. She is also a visual artist, and teaches workshops in many aspects of writing, culture, communication, and creativity.

Shirley McPhillips, Poet Laureate for Choice Literacy, is author of *Acrylic Angel of Fate; Poem Central: Word Journeys with Readers and Writers*; and, with Nick Flynn, *A Note Slipped Under the Door: Teaching from Poems We Love*. Her poetry was honored at the Artists Embassy International Dancing Poetry Festival, 2017, in San Francisco, CA.

Dr. Amanda Morris is an Associate Professor of writing and rhetoric at Kutztown University of Pennsylvania, the co-creator and co-host of Inside 254 Podcast, and developer of a new online writing course called Write Your Life Story: Getting Started. She has over 20 years of experience as a published writer.

Patricia A. Nugent is the author of *They Live On: Saying Goodbye to Mom and Dad*, a compilation of vignettes and poems about losing a loved one. Previously published in trade and literary journals, she's currently working on her second manuscript entitled *Healing with Dolly Lama: Finding God in Dog*.

Richard Parisio lives and writes in the Hudson Valley, where he works as a naturalist and educator. He has been NYS Coordinator for *River of Words*, a children's watershed poetry program, since 2002. Parisio's collection, *The Owl Invites Your Silence*, won the 2014 Slapering Hol Press Poetry Chapbook Award.

Kay Peters' poems have been published in *Philadelphia Poets, U.S.1 Worksheets, Apiary, Mad Poets Review*, and *Schuylkill Valley Journal*. Kay is a Registered Nurse and a former Oncology Clinical Nurse Specialist who now practices as a parish nurse.

Wanda S. Praisner received the Egan Award, Princemere Prize, Kudzu Award, First Prize in Poetry at the College of NJ Writers' Conference, and the 2017 New Jersey Poets Prize. She appears in *Atlanta Review, Lullwater Review*, and *Prairie Schooner*. Her fifth collection is *Natirar* (Kelsay Books, 2017). She's a poet for the state.

Dorothy Ryan's poems have appeared in *America* (she was a finalist for the Foley Prize), *The Christian Science Monitor, Stillwater Review, Naugatuck River Review, Paterson Literary Review*, and *The Pedestal*, among others, including anthologies. Her chapbook is *Animal Weaver* (Carpenter Press 2002). She is working on a collection of poems.

Christine E. Salvatore received her MFA from The University of New Orleans. She currently teaches at Stockton University, in the MFA Program at Rosemont College, and at a public high school in South Jersey. When she's not working, she hangs out with her dog, Lady Brett Ashley, and her boyfriend, Lee.

Taylor Carmen Savath is a writer, speaker, and activist who has spoken at conferences for disabled students and their families all over the east coast. These experiences, along with being an active member of a local poetry community, offer her a unique perspective from which to write.

Mimi Schwartz's new book, *When History Is Personal*, includes this essay as one of 25 that explore connections between her experience and the world that shapes them (March 2018, University of Nebraska Press). Other books include: *Thoughts from a Queen-Sized Bed; Good Neighbors, Bad Times*; and *Writing True: The Art and Craft of Creative Nonfiction*.

David Simpson's poetry collection, *The Way Love Comes to Me*, was published by MutualMuse Books in 2014. With grants from The Independence Foundation and the National Endowment for the Arts, he wrote *Crossing the Threshold into the House of Bach*, a one-person play produced in 2015 by Amaryllis Theatre, Philadelphia.

Jeanne Sutton: Omnivorous bookworm. Insatiably curious. Indefatigable journal-keeper. Passionate poet, public reader of. Occasional actress. Laughter self-medicator. Good ghostwriter. Frequent freelancer. Clever copywriter. Efficient editor. Honest essayist. Published novelist, *Blood Sisters, Antoinette*. Former wife, proud mom, grateful gran. Lately? Inspired Getaway go-er, delusional-ly challenged, writing own things.

J. C. Todd, the 2016 Rita Dove Poetry Prize winner, holds fellowships from the Pew Foundation, Pennsylvania Council on the Arts, Ucross, and Ragdale. Publications include *What Space This Body*, an artist-book collaboration titled *FUBAR*, and poems in *APR*, *Paris Review*, and *Beloit Poetry Journal*. She is on the MFA faculty at Rosemont.

Kim Mary Trotto is a retired journalist. Three of her stories are published in webzines and her horror story, "The Gold Fish," grown from a prompt seed provided by Peter Murphy, was published in the print magazine, *Luna Station*. Kim has also written feature stories and essays for local newspapers.

Pat Valdata is an award-winning poet and novelist. Her publications include two novels, two books of poetry, and a chapbook. She teaches creative writing online for the University of Maryland University College (UMUC) and lives in Crisfield, Maryland.

John Wojtowicz grew up working on his family's azalea and rhododendron nursery in the backwoods of South Jersey. He is currently employed as a social worker and takes every opportunity to combine this work with his passion for wilderness. Besides poetry, he likes bonfires, boots, and bluegrass.

Evan Yavne holds a Master's Degree in Teaching from NYU, where he was awarded a fellowship, and has taught Middle School English and college level English and writing courses. He owns Solar Alchemy, Inc., a solar design and installation company, and currently teaches renewable energy courses in Ulster County, NY.

Acknowledgments

Copyrights to the poems, stories, and essays collected in this book belong to the authors. They have graciously given us permission to include their work.

Kim Addonizio: "To the Woman Crying Uncontrollably in the Next Stall" from *The Night Could Go in Either Direction*, with Brittany Perham, Slapering Hol Press, 2016. Reprinted in *Diode Poetry Journal*, Spring 2016, volume 9, number 1.

JoAnn Balingit: "In the Stirrups" originally published in *Poemeleon*, Volume IX: The Asian Pacific American Issue, Spring 2017.

Norma Ketzis Bernstock: "11:00 PM in Price Chopper" originally published in The River Reporter's *Literary Gazette*, April 2016.

Shirley J. Brewer: "Goddess of the Second Hand" from *Bistro in Another Realm*, Main Street Rag, 2017. Originally published in *Spillway*, 2015.

Jin Cordaro: "My Husband Is Burning," originally published in *Faultline*, Issue 22, 2013.

Barbara Daniels: "Winter Swim," originally published in *Casa de Cinco Hermanas*, Volume 13, 2013.

Emari DiGiorgio: "The Grand Opera of Boko Haram," from *Girl Torpedo*, AGAPE editions, 2018. Originally published in *HEArt*, February 2016 and winner of the 2016 Woodrow Hall Top Shelf Award.

Karen Z Duffy: "I Am Silenced for the First Time in Twenty-Four Years," originally published in *The Journal of New Jersey Poets*, 2009, Issue 46.

Sandy Gingras: "Poof" from *Not Even Close to What She Planned On*, Diode Editions, 2015. Originally published in *New Ohio Review*, 2014, Issue 16.

Ona Gritz: "Home, I Say" from *Geode*, Main Street Rag, 2014. Originally published in *Literary Mama*, January 2006.

Robert Halleck: "Hugs No Kisses," originally published in *The Lake*, May 2017. Reprinted in *Shot Glass Journal*, Issue 22, May 2017.

Peter Krok: "They Visit Her Eyes," originally published in *Muddy River Poetry Review*, Spring 2017.

Dorianne Laux: "Chair," originally published in *Oxford American*, Issue 86, Fall 2014.

Marcia LeBeau: "Letter to Myself at Eighty," forthcoming in *Painted Bride Quarterly*, Issue 96.

Kay Peters: "Close Cut," originally published in *Philadelphia Stories*, Winter 2015.

Wanda Praisner: "Early Morning" from *Sometimes When Something Is Singing*, Antrim House, 2014. Originally published in *Prairie Schooner*, Spring 2012.

Mimi Schwartz: "Story on a Winter Beach" from *When History is Personal*, University of Nebraska Press, forthcoming, March 2018. Originally published in *New Jersey Monthly*, June 2002, as "Sharing Stories."

David Simpson: "Grace" from *The Way Love Comes to Me*, MutualMuse Books, 2014.

Jeanne Sutton: "Sister-in-Lawhood," originally published in *Minerva Rising*, Issue 11, Fall 2016.

Pat Valdata: "Renovations," originally published in *Little Patuxent Review*, Winter 2013.

John Wojtowicz: "Mr. Moon," originally published in *Naugatuck River Review*, Summer/Fall 2016.

With gratitude to:

Peter Murphy, Amanda Murphy Kumpas, and Taylor Coyle for the amazing gift of the Winter Poetry & Prose Getaway and for entrusting us with this project; Patty Paine and Law Alsobrook for making this book a beautiful, physical thing; and the writers who generously shared their work with us.

Editor Bios

Ona Gritz is the author of two poetry collections, two children's books, and a memoir. Her work has appeared in *The New York Times, the Guardian, Ploughshares*, and elsewhere. She and Daniel Simpson were co-poetry editors for *Referential Magazine*. Their joint collection, *Border Songs*, is available from Finishing Line Press.

Daniel Simpson's *School for the Blind* was published by Poets Wear Prada (2014). He and Ona Gritz co-authored *Border Songs: A Conversation in Poems* (Finishing Line Press, 2017), and collaborated as poetry editors for *Referential Magazine. The New York Times* and numerous poetry magazines have printed his work. He blogs at insidetheinvisible.wordpress.com.

Peter E. Murphy has been leading workshops for writers and teachers since 1981. He is the author of *Stubborn Child* – a finalist for the Paterson Poetry Prize – five poetry chapbooks, and hundreds of essays and poems published in literary journals. He is the founder of Murphy Writing of Stockton University.